EMOTIONAL
RAGS TO
SPIRITUAL
RICHES

"Addiction is a gift to the rebirthing of the soul"

June —
You ARE ALWAYS BOTH
SO WELCOME HERE

David Stanley Gregory

ISBN 978-1-954345-31-7 (paperback)
ISBN 978-1-954345-37-9 (hardcover)
ISBN 978-1-954345-38-6 (digital)

Rushmore Press LLC
1 800 460 9188
www.rushmorepress.com

Printed in the United States of America

Chapter One

What We Get Is What We Think

DOESN'T EVERYONE LOVE AND RELATE *to a great "rags to riches" story?* Since the movie industry began, these stories have not only gotten top billing in movie houses, they are usually best sellers at the local bookstore. *And, why shouldn't they be?* We all like to think that we can pull ourselves out of a sinkhole, and end up on a mountaintop. And, we can.

However, living in the throes of emotional rags, and trying to get out of a sinkhole can cause us to experience a great deal of fear. *How can we magically transform our emotional rags into spiritual riches?* This is especially true, when we create stores and screenplays based on past and future fears and deficiencies. As a result, we can become hesitant to move forward in our lives. We become frustrated, and many times we feel hopeless and "wanting."

A good story about "rags to riches" is often glorified at the movies, but when we go to the theatre, or sit at home pondering dilemmas, we face that clear-cut reality that we made. These dilemmas remind us that our lives will never change. In other words, we will never truly have what we really need. *Why?* Well, because we are not worthy to receive such gifts. In fact, many of us accept life for what we THINK it is, and not what it could be, if we were willing to change the way we think. It is our thoughts that influence what happens in our lives.

But, first we must realize that our depression and hopelessness is a learned a behavior. *The question now is, regardless of where we are now in our lives…do we want to have more in life? Do we want to be more life? Are we ready to do the next right thing to have what was destined for us?* Or, have we decided to surrender to a power less than ourselves, when there is a power greater than ourselves, who is ready to give us the life we have been…just as long as we do this one thing. In other words, we need to change everything in order to have the life we want. It can be done, but it must be undertaken one step at time, one day at time, and one moment at a time. We must live in the NOW.

Truth-be-told, we all experience "emotional rags" at certain times in our lives. We may also have financial challenges, or there may be circumstances that strip away our peace, leaving us trapped within our heads. In addition, we may fail in our relationships, or be abandoned by our families. And, then, there is always the sadness of losing a loved one. But, the biggest tiger in the woods is change. We find that change takes us out of our peaceful states, and causes us to become paralyzed with fear - unable to think, do, or be. For many of us, change is bigger than death, or financial insecurities. In fact, none one is immune to life's "ups and downs," "turns and curves," and "stops and starts."

Yes, our lives are similar to many others with varying degrees of the "ups and downs." *So, what is life on life's terms? Is it possible to connect with our higher selves? What if the grand prize, when dealing with adversities, is doing the right thing? What opportunities do we need to seek to discard adversities?* We always know. It lives quietly within us. But, many times we need a nudge, or a trigger, or a disaster to bring us to our senses in the NOW of our lives.

Life IS. Life is totally connected to the truth of our spiritual essence - the real us. Our souls are who we are. Our minds help us learn and observe on a soulful level. When life is solely on life's terms, without a connection to our spiritual side, it places us in the trenches of despair. There is no open road to our spiritual riches, especially if we succumb to despair by not using our God-given spiritual nature to release, and change our adverse experiences. In our despair, the flip side IS our opportunities. This wakeup call always comes at a point in our lives, when we recognize that we are a "soul" of many choices.

We may not always take the opportunity, as our egos still want to be in control, convincing us that we have all the answers. And, we do. But, not from the chatter of the many messages that bring us past, present, and future doubts, fears, and regrets. We will, however, continue to receive messages that feel "right." Once that occurs we will need to decipher what we have been observing, and what "right" thing we should do next. Emotional rags are the vehicles to spiritual riches. *The choice is always ours.*

In this state of peaked awareness, we may gain a realization that there is a significant difference between chattering egos, and the deep, warm knowing of our hearts. At least we can realize, while in that state of awareness that it is time to start making decisions. However, even with good intentions, unless we are ready to move out of our emotional rags story, chances are we will have little reprieve, if any. And, then there are some of us, who think that we can go it alone, but with choices, we try to make life happen on our own terms. We may even forfeit valuable help from our Higher Power. And, as a result, we can't receive the messages that will help us manifest the riches we are seeking. The universe is friendly, kind, and ready, as soon as we make our way towards turning our rags to riches.

Fear, at times, can motivate us at certain times during our journeys. In fact, fear used to be a tool of the ego (to get us out of dangerous situations). But, as we have evolved, it has become more than a voice to get us out of fearful situations. Fear has actually evolved with our ego to scare us from living out our lives, and co-creating with the God of our understanding. It is important to understand that emotional rags are caused by fear. The rags will continue to multiply, until we learn how to change the way we think. Our thoughts encourage the "good" and "bad" in our lives. If emotional rags are laced with fearful decisions that prevent us from moving forward, we are sacrificing our spiritual riches until we learn "fearless living" in the NOW. This is a story of our emotional rags. *So, what does fear sound like? Are we even able to recognize it, or are we so used to "fearful living" that it is second nature to us?* Fear IS. Fear IS just like Peace IS. It is recognizing the relentless chatter of our egos.

We get stopped in our tracks. Something happens to wake us up. We become our own story. We either want to keep it, or we want to change it. A story that could turn out to be a happy ending laced with fear becomes the story of who we are. *Fearful.* But, if we want to dispel the fear, we can, at any point, release it to something bigger and greater, then we are. Once released, the fog lifts, the mask is removed, and the answers revealed. Releasing the fear is a spiritual richness that is immediately felt with a deep calming breath of relief. We are breathing again, and not holding our breaths.

Spiritual riches explode with a constant gift of rebirthing. Once we have been tempted, and teased with such wonderful life gifts, we never want to let them go. And, even though fear lurks in a secret disguise, once exposed (because of truth and transparency), we are immediately set free to move on with a confidence that we are on track. Our obsessive egos now have the spiritual power needed to "let go." It is important to remember that "letting go" creates a change that prompts us, if we listen to it. "Change is change only."

Once again, we are in the mode of making a choice. We can accept the adversity, and return the fear, or we can seek opportunities, and allow our altered thinking patterns to become a life-changing positive experience. In other words, there is no risk in changing because "change" is always "changing." There is also no risk in accepting the "change," moving through it, and finding out what we need to know, as we make our way through the process. "Change" is not even a calculated risk. We cannot calculate something that will happen anyways.

So, we can count on one thing, our entire life – "change." The quicker we accept opportunities to "change," the quicker we are able to do what we need to do. We stop putting our lives on hold, and fighting the inevitable. Wow, that is asking us to do a lot of changing. *What if we are not ready for "change?"* Well, it is ready for us, and it plans to guide us to the lives we are destined to live. We can fight it, but there should be no judging, especially if we decide not to go with the flow of "change." However, we may feel that we are missing out. Then, we will begin to regret, in our NOW moments, not accomplishing what we could have accomplished. Our Higher Power does not judge our inability to change - but we do. Self-judgments are extremely hard because our human conditions take longer to forgive ourselves for not showing up fully in our lives.

Once shot out of the cannon of "change," we are overwhelmed with spiritual riches. We immediately start to learn, and recognize what is working for us, and what is not. We are then prepared, and ready to live in our NOW fully. We are finally showing up in our lives. *We feel good.* We are not stagnating. Rather, we listen for our next move into nirvana - an arena of peaceful knowledge that may not be used, but still gives us immediate comfort. We may even wonder why we have stayed so connected to the fear of change, and the future projections that we allow our egos to chat about. Well, with this loss of fear comes an automatic "richness of faith." Some call this a faith in God, but it must start with a faith in ourselves. That is faith. More specifically, once we accept the fact that faith has a shadow twin brother called fear and it will not live long in our emotions; this is especially true if we have faith in God. This is also true, once we experience the spiritual richness of faith. But, it takes the emotional rags for us to find a way to experience the faith that is needed to catapult us into spiritual riches.

Money and the gifts do not have to be our life stories. But, money does trigger fear - fear of not having our needs met, or not having our needs met enough. But, why not ask ourselves this question - *Will we ever have "enough," and will we ever be happy and content with what we have? Or, does more stimulate the need for more?*

When we move on, we move in relationships. We, once again, take the "low road of fear," by choosing to be fearful, and as a result, we are unable to obtain what we need. Or, maybe we really do have what we need, but just want more just like we want more of everything else in our lives. The presenting-self pops up, which is what we show to the world. *What will people think? What do they know about me? What do I need to hide?* Now, we hide our lives from those, who know us, by not being authentic. A life of fear prevents us from getting what we truly want in a partner. Fear also causes us to be afraid of running out of the money we need to survive.

We have chosen lives that are not available to "richness," in any form. It will take an act of providence for us to change our thinking patterns. But, no worries...it will come, as it always does. We just need to recognize it when it shows up. Truthfully, most us want to ignore the signs. But, under duress, we are forced to look at ourselves, and make a choice. *Do we want to stay where we are, or go on?* If finances are a primary contender for fear in our life stories, there may be so much fear of loss, or possible loss, that we become paralyzed with fear all over again. But, by this time, in this ongoing process, we should be able to double back quickly, grab our faith in ourselves, and show up and/or move into our NOW with spiritual our armor in place. And, even when faced with old thoughts that keep us in past, and current rags of emotional drama, there are times in our lives when emotional situations, such as: a loss of money, a job, a relationship, and/or family and friends remain stuck in our heads. Our egos haunt us. They perpetuate our past and future histories that continue to haunt us relentlessly.

These are also times where egoist monkey "mind chatter" takes center court in our rented courtroom. In other words, we believe that we don't have a good defensive to fight our vicious perpetrators. It has taken hold of our minds, and refuses to let up, or so we think. We are in the "Yet" of "letting up." These messages prevent us from peace. There is a need to access the "voice of surrender" – the voice that lives within us - the voice that knows how to battle an out-of-control ego.

Once again opportunity appears, when connecting to the voice within. To find the voice that will set us free is only a thought away. This is our chance to exercise the power of listening. In other words, we become "observers," who are merely "observing" chattering egos. At this point, we can choose to "observe," without participation, as if we are watching a game or movie. This is our opportunity to detach from the power, and listen to the core of our hearts. This is the next "right" thing to do. To clarify, a bounty supply of spiritual riches is available during our present moments.

When we are ready to grow, even if we are not aware of it, a positive message like: "shit happens" comes to mind. That small voice within us has been working overtime for a long time, and playing to an empty house. That real voice that has the answer does not give up. It comes through in small increments of messages or one big loud…"HEY YOU!" Fortunately, the messages garner attention, which occurs every time you start to grow. Living in the NOW, and finding our authenticity and transparency are two important tools that we must show up.

"Change" is eminent, so even if we are in the throes of depression, anger, fear, we still have the opportunities we have been subconsciously waiting for. In other words, the universe is very powerful. And, being that we are part of that powerful energy indicates just how powerful we are too - once we resist the separation, and realize the "oneness" in all things. It is important to understand that we will get nudges in our lives. But, these nudges give us the information and the guidance that we need to live and find the happiness we desire. But, we must choose it, and *SHOW UP!*

Spiritual riches coexist with us. In fact, they are readily available once we delete our emotional rags. They jump up and down, and wiggle and squirm deep within us, as a method to escape the grips of the egos. When this time arrives, the spiritual riches knock at our door. *Will you let yours in?*

It takes guts and bravery to surrender our old ways of thinking, but once you are able to do that, spiritual riches can barge into your life.

Emotional rags are the catalyst to spiritual riches. *Who would have guessed it could be so straightforward? Why me O'Lord… Why Me?* Once we understand this concept, we can say, *"Why not me?"* We will never know light until we know darkness. We will never know up until we recognize down. The "yins and yangs" of life have purpose. *So, what are those purposes?*

One of the first noticeable signs of emotional rags is that we feel, as if our energy has been zapped! *Well, it has.* Our energy is so compromised that we have no idea what riches we need to feel complete, in regards to success, prosperity, and peaceful living.

The quest is to understand that opportunities live within us. In other words, living externally means that we are separate from everything and everyone around us. *If we are separate, then who can possibly help us? Who will possibly care about what we need?* If this is true, our energy will be stagnate, because there will be no need to intertwine and mesh with anything on the planet. *But, that is not so.* We are all connected. We need each other to survive. We live with a Higher Power, whether we recognize it or not. In other words, there is an energy that lives within us that is in everything that we do, hear, smell, touch and see. So, take a moment, and look at the NOW. *What is in the NOW that is not in everyone that you meet?* We are connected, so the sooner we accept that we are, the sooner we will, once again, be blessed with spiritual riches. The emotional rags that bring us to our spiritual riches do not have a chance of surviving, once we accept that we are all connected.

However, it takes a spiritual treasure hunt. Hopefully, we will realize that the treasure is not hidden from us, just eluding us, until we are ready to accept it. We will get many clues and nudges, and sometimes we will also get nagged, and feel broken, before we find our riches. *But, they are there.* They have always been there. We will find them, if we pose the question, *"Where are they?"* And, by listening to the small voices in our heads, we will get our answer. The universe never misses a question, a phone call, a test, or request.

However, once we have surrendered to the fact that we need to find our treasure, we will find that the hunt is exciting and full of surprises. *When that occurs, we have moved into the NOW.* In that moment, we will be showered with a richness of just knowing that we have moved into a new dimension. We are now free to listen. We are ready to let go of old antiquated ideas that we picked up along the way. Our pasts have faded away. Our futures hold promise. *We are connected.*

Showing up to the hunt is foremost in finding the information need to experience a full revelation and acquire our spiritual riches. We will be amazed to realize that our spiritual riches have never been in hiding, and have always been in plain view. We were blinded by unhealthy egos, and the thought patterns that correspond with those cunning enemies of the heart. It is always prudent to remember how devious and cunning egos are. An ego is a rag that is willing to halt discoveries on the path to spiritual riches. Egos cannot withstand truth, fear, or authentic NOW thinking patterns. They retreat quickly. But, do not be fooled, as egos patiently await patiently opportunities to trigger fearful chatters.

A path to spiritual riches needs a plan, and most importantly, it needs a "willingness" to get search for the treasure by moving in the right direction. Truthfully, we may find that our lives have been somewhat of a train wreck. However, getting off the train, and never boarding another one doesn't work either.

We need a train that is going somewhere. Our new destination is calling us. Why not climb back on the next train, and get started with the journey that has been calling us for a long time. It is a natural feeling take an in-depth look at what we are doing. It is also natural to bypass something that we want. In other words, most of us have a habit of finding too many excuses, triggered by fear and doubt. But, there is a thrill in the looking…then finding the story that tells us how we got here.

Are we one of the talented souls that is up for the journey or are we one of those souls that suffers from the journey? Do we think about all the "ifs?" And, should we allow the "shoulds" to come into play, as contenders in our egos? If we are ready, we will reach our final destination of *NIRVANA,* and there will be no need of "what ifs" or "shoulds." And, as with all journeys, there will always be more lands to discover…more *NIRVANAS* on the horizon. Once we delete the negative responses from our heads, our trip will become one of sightseeing, instead of just a destination. In other words, our journeys will be softer, easier, and more comfortable. *Why?*

Well, because we will know that we are guided and loved. And, we will be championed by our angels, guides, and loved ones. The cheering section will be everywhere we go. We will be welcomed into the fold with open arms. The seekers will get their treasures in the form of spiritual riches. On the other hand, the stay-at-home folks will get to stay at home, and suffer with emotional rags. *It's a choice… it's all a choice.*

More specifically, when we understand that we need to identify the emotional rags in order to have the spiritual riches, we are more than half way there. The riches arise with ease and grace, but only if we are willing. There are no secrets to "having it all." We cannot have everything, but we can have it all - that is - all that we choose to journey through, and with.

Many of us need a nudge to get our journeys going. It can be a hard nudge or a soft nudge, depending on where we are in our thought processes. The universe knows when, and how to get our attention.

Some of us are fortunate, and have not experienced the deep despair of emotional rags that are born from addiction, suicide, and/or suicidal thoughts. Others have to go through passive aggressive relationships, and/or thoughtless and selfish lives. If that's what it takes, that's what it takes. But, something has to get our attention.

However, we are not judged by a loving universe, or if you will, the God of our understanding. The universe always welcomes us when we are ready to engage with this wonderful thing called life. We have come out of a long period of sleepwalking. And, being that most of us are prodigal at one time or another, coming home to a soulful life, is a welcoming experience. We find that we are on our way home, to either this life or the next. Coming home is an ongoing walk. It is a time to show up. In fact, showing up is the first step to participating in an abundant and well-organized, thoughtful universe - that is always on time.

There will be times, when we observe others, and feel that they are fortunate to have found a way of living that seems to serve them well. It is futile and energy stealing to compare yourself with others. Everyone puts his or her time in…or not. Coming into this life from a previous life may make this time a little clearer, and not so difficult. But, by not comparing yourself to another person's journey, we learn to show up to our own lives. We also learn how to find available answers that enlighten us when the darkness approaches. During this time it is important to look towards to the light to find the answers and to calm our restless spirits.

ONENESS of our spiritual connection is always within us, at our side, and by adding a beam of light to an existing light that has been dimmed or out; we are able to realize the importance of being connecting to the world around us. Oneness is important for recognizing that we are not living in a universe of separation. In other words, everything that we need is always available. More specifically, if we are centered and quiet, we can hear our helpful guides directing our every move. During this time, we are out of our heads, and feeling the energy around us. And, by being aware of this, we will not miss this powerful experience.

If we are struggling, and cannot get out of our heads, there will be another time for powerful experiences to display themselves. A friendly universe of spiritual riches patiently awaits us - waiting to gift us our rite of passage.

Our personal journeys, if done well, or not done well, will have an effect on everyone that we come into contact with. We are lessons for some people, and healing for others. So, when we find a formula to help us get from emotional rags to spiritual riches, we happily give away the formula to others - that this is our way of making sure we keep our gifts.

Once we heal our own emotional rags, we become part of the total healing equation of how other souls will be accepting, and witness through us the vast amounts of spiritual riches. *We are walking our talk.* We have proven to ourselves, as well as to others, that in order to become available to our spiritual riches, we must choose a life that discards ways of living that are no longer useful. It is true that emotional rags have their necessary place. *What is their place?* Well, it is to lead us to the spiritual riches.

We call it a new path, but are we not returning to an old path? Like light, our paths have always been there. It just IS, and there will always be the Light. We now recognize that darkness is only a lack of light. The path is our light. We see it when we choose our accelerated path. There are plenty of spiritual riches to go around, so in order to keep what we have, there must be requirements. In other words, we are here to share good, so that we can keep our goodness. We are getting more centered, therefore, we no longer react or over-react to the people we love, or the people we causally interact with.

During this time, we experience a oneness principle to the point that we are recognize that we are "one" with the universe and the universe is everything. What does this mean for us? Well, we no longer feel a separation from God, Man, Plants, and Animals etc. We are learning to feel the universe as an spiritual gold mind to have and share with others. Others will be amazed at how comfortable we are in our own skins. Most everyone wants to have a feeling of belonging to a force that does not separate them from their goodness. Most of us want an opportunity to find a path of healing in specific areas of their lives. This information and way of living has never been held in secret. Sages and monks, and all of us have the right to find our spiritual riches. The rags have de-toured us from the path to recover our riches. Sages may sit in silence longer, and monks may hibernate in the hills, but we all get to have the formula of how to find our spiritual riches. As is true under the universal law of cause and effect…it takes what it takes. First, we must know our emotional rags, and then, we will be ready to discover the riches we will receive from a life that embraces every moment of every day.

We all have periods, in which we just cannot get the formula to work with our inner selves. *We want what we what, and we want it now.* We obsess over the riches. *What are the riches we are seeking? Are they the ones that rust or fade, or have a temporary life cycle? Or, are they timeless, traveling with us through eternity?* Do not be discouraged with the formula because our riches will always be on time. They may not be on our time, but they will be on "perfect time" with all that we are, and all that we do.

There is more involved to receiving spiritual riches than just ourselves. There will be others, who join in to be part of these spiritual riches. *And, it is well worth the wait.* If we push the water to get what we want, we could easily drown in the undertow. We will know when our time has come. There will be that certain feeling that certain nudge. Our inner guides will bolt into action, and show us the way. We will feel the difference, and then, we will see what is happening with a spiritual third eye.

Our guides will never let up on us, just as the God of our understanding never lets us go. There may be a waiting period, as we prepare for what is to come, but we will never be abandoned. We could slip back into the same old ways as we get closer to learning what it takes to be ready for the gifts of living in our NOW. Old ways are full of the same old results. *But, is this not the part of the journey that gets our attention, and puts us back on track?*

We once again realize that our road has been traveled this way before, but now we have new information. By repeating old emotional rags, we slip back into to old patterns, and once again repeating old behaviors. We have unintentionally detached from the spiritual richness that we finally came to know. And, because we are once again caught in our heads, and not listening to our hearts, we forget about the tools we use to stay present in our NOW. No worries...we get to try as many times as we choose to return to the sanity of what we have already learned.

Once we have good sound knowledge of what we asked for, and what we are seeking, the universe is not quite as forgiving. In fact, we tend to feel uncomfortable once we realize that we are not living up to the truth of what we have been given for a better, more focused life. This is a life of service not just to ourselves, but also to everyone we come in contact with. We become connected in a way that we have never been before. In addition, it no longer takes an extended time and/or multiple lessons to figure it all out. The discomfort of not showing up to what we know actually becomes our best motivator to keep us moving. We are stopped much more quickly, once we have repeated unhealthy behaviors.

This is an emotional rag that cannot live long in our consciousness. Even our egos have little to chatter about once we have conquered a lesson, and are ready to move on. We will receive direct pointed messages that let us know to resume our path and stay on track. *All and all, this is good.* There is no need to sit in an old lesson for long. There will come many indicators, out of the blue, to put us back on track.

Once we realize that we are doing things the same old ways, or hopefully the same new ways, we actually attract a likeminded moment to what we are thinking. Everything we want and need manifests the thought processes required to stay focused on what we want to manifest. We always make something happen, and that is why we need to monitor our thoughts. We are a magnet to thoughts. Our thoughts manifest within us. *What is a great question to ask ourselves?*

A positive universe only know positives, which means that our thoughts, regardless of what we are thinking, remain a positive flow of energy; to re-emphasize the point - we get what we think in some form or another. *Why?* Well, because the universe is a positive source of energy. For example, it is a wise person, who is careful with his or her words, and thoughts. To observe our thinking patterns is the key to catch the truth before it eludes us with a brazen off the cuff remark stimulated by our unhealthy egos. So, with care, and the lesson of learning to listen to our soulful selves, we are able to have positive thoughts, and knowledge of what we are manifesting for the greater good, starting with ourselves.

Most of us, who have come to believe that we are spiritual beings, living an earthly life, have experienced the power of prayer. Many of us feel we know how to ask for what we need; but with the power of prayer and spiritual richness, there is another step that assures our success. We would be good to affirm that the prayer has already been answered, and then let it go with a knowing that the God of our understanding will manifest this request at the right time, in the right place, and with the right people involved. And, as we affirm our prayers we allow our thoughts of good intentions to manifest. The simplicity of knowing that our thoughts are prayers will help us listen to what we are saying. This is just one more way to tether the ego, and observe our prayers.

Changing our thinking patterns is the biggest on-going gift we can acquire, and continue to give us. We will come to know that our old ways of life have imprisoned our true and authentic selves. We are signed up to be students that never stop learning; as we begin by knowing that what we think and learn is a process leading to our highest levels of spiritual existence.

It is definitely a process to be in this thing called life. Some of us show up for the big stuff, and some of us wait until later. But, in the end, no matter how long it takes, we will all be moving on, and getting there at the pace that was decided in another lifetime. We can choose to do our best or learn to do our best over and over again. Some of us need the repetition, and others want to move on quickly after a lesson is achieved. It doesn't matter how we individually get there because we are all ONE in all things. We are yin and yang. We give and take. We come to understand that being alive in this lifetime is an opportunity to become more of who we are. We will evolve, if we do the next right thing in this lifetime. If we do not, it is still not over...the Fat Lady has not sung. Her vibrato is unrelenting throughout eternity. In essence the song is never over.

We get a choice to view lesson as either good or bad. Truthfully, we are all about choices. Depending on how we have addressed and changed our thinking patterns, our similar situations, and old lessons may keep coming up. They may also grab our attention as many times as necessary, until we make the choice to heal or not to heal. There is no drug, no amount of alcohol, and no addiction out there that will allow us to hide our lessons, and true selves for long. We will be put on notice with a form of physical and/or emotional pain. This emotional rag is our opening to address our souls. Every soul is alike in that it has the potential to have, do, and be everything it is here to accomplish.

There may have been a time when we were allowed to check out, while still under protection of our consequences, but with the wake-up call of addiction, of any kind, there comes a day when it stops working. And, no matter how hard one tries to escape the soul's journey through addiction, surrender is the only spiritual richness that will save us from this emotional rag. Our old behaviors are worn out, and no longer work. *Not anymore.* We have crossed the line, and now feel the pain, which hopefully brings us to our senses.

We find ourselves nudged with whatever it takes to help us come into our NOW and become ONE with who and what we are here to do. This is not an easy or planned surrender. It is our last breath before change. It is our only hope of survival. Our real work of showing up has just begun. We are in a re-birthing process, even in our discontentment, and our willingness most often is to not yet be willing. It may take a couple more times of extreme pain, before we stay fixed firmly on the knees of surrender.

Upon re-grouping through surrender, and working on letting go of emotional rags, we become ready to accept our spiritual riches. They come to us freely and with ease. We find that we want to have the riches of spiritual existence. We have always been spiritual, but hesitant to come forward, and enjoy the possibilities that go with belonging to a universe of ONENESS. We are the cause. Therefore, we create the effect of everything we do. The laws of cause and effect are now working in our best interest, not like before where we caused negative effects in our lives.

Sometimes in our stubbornness to change, we bypass intuition. Our intuition is our God within, when properly tapped and listened to.

We would rather put all of our energy into ignoring the emotional rags we are dragging with us. Silently and painfully like a martyr, we accept the emotional rags, and carry them, as if we were victims of circumstance. And, we are…our own circumstances. Our dramas hit heights that are obvious to all and oblivious to us. We are wearing life, as if we were pushing a mountain that will not budge, or wearing spandex two sizes too small. We have not found loose garments that allow us to flow with the "ebbs and tides" of our lives. We are tight until we are not. We are not present to anything, until we are. Our unhealthy chattering egos drown out all messages of well-being until we shut it down, and learn how to send it away in a moment's notice.

Our valiant victim-hoods, we own for as long as we choose to live in a world of separation. With our chins jutting out in defiance, we conclude that we are here to live out our dramas and fears. What a pity party we have created for ourselves, yet how stubborn we are when it comes to changing our thinking patterns, so that our chins drops to a normal, comfortable position. Only then a smile can emerge.

No matter how we live...happy or defiant, depressed or fearful, alone or boisterous, we will always be the stars of our own shows. There is no one that has the exact same entrance and exits as us. We write our own scripts, we are the directors, making changes, and we sponsor ourselves (or choose not to), and then, we live out our emotional rags until we come to the conclusion that we are ready for our spiritual riches. We may have doubts and fears, but being a "Doubting Thomas" will prevent us from moving to the next level. But, in the end, we are granted every opportunity possible to embrace all the spiritual richness known to man. We take what we need, and leave the rest. We are the "choosers" of our destinies, and like it or not, we are living it right NOW.

If we have chosen to live our lives at a level of low energy, our outward actions will tell our stories to the world. We tell the world, without even muttering a word, just how bad we think we have it. We ask others to watch us or at the very least try to participate by taking a closer look at the albatross, we have willfully tied around our necks. The high drama is apparent. In fact, we are only attracting high drama. The only ones listening to our woes are the ones, who dramatize along with us about our own lives. It definitely becomes a choice of consciousness or unconsciousness. But, we are the ones that make our own choices.

Then, there are those of us, who hide in our emotions by staying noticeably quiet. We choose to be stealth. We are watchers, who stay in the background with little to say, as being invisible allows us not to participate in life. *What risk is there to being invisible?* Being invisible is like a groundhog, without his shadow. No one gets to decide how to love, or honor a person that is invisible. They bring neither goodness nor badness to the table of life. But, someday, when they see their shadows, the invisible ones will be scared away. No one is ever left out when discovering the soul's journey, and why we are here. We can ignore it, but time will reveal it, even if we choose not to share it. So, the time comes when the invisible is very visible. God IS and God IS everywhere. The soul will emerge, and when that happens there will be an emergence that will define the lifetime of our souls.

Egos can disguise our souls with various personalities and masks. Their tendencies to drink and drug, along with any other kind of addictive behaviors, can sidetrack our emotional rags, but in the end…we must emerge to the God of our understanding, no matter what we call this Higher Being. Our higher consciousness always wins, either in this lifetime or the next.

Addictions have a place for a certain amount of time. For example, a person needing to hold on to their emotional rags, in the form of addictions, may do so because they lack trust and faith in something greater than themselves. These souls seek out anything that is mind and mood altering. They do not want to conflict with their egos and hearts. And, when the battle begins, as it always does, the addictions quiet the hearts and heads. No decisions are made. No wealth of spiritual riches is received.

We shop until we drop, drink until we pass out, drug ourselves into "La-La Land," eat until we can't move, and/or use sex as a temporary fix, but the fix is always short - temporary. And, then, the day comes, and it is no longer a suitable "fix." But, until then, from one fix to the next, we seek anything and everything that allows us not to think, listen, or heal.

Our defiance is the emotional rag used to score our next quick fix. Addictive behaviors work for a while, but eventually become noticeably tempered with varied degrees of "bottoming out." This is needed to get our attention.

Many have never wakened from this insanity; rather, they have simply lost everything, and then died. Sometimes, death is their way of transitioning out of this life, and other times they die, while they are living. They are walking death without the mental capacities to participate in life.

The finale aka the end of a life, as we know it, comes to a screeching halt. And, if we catch it in time, we can produce the "PHOENIX RISING EFFECT." And, out of the ashes comes a rebirth…a living breathing resurrection that is seen by all. It is a starting over point but a starting over where we left off point. We are not just starting over. We are starting again, but this time with the willingness to change the way we think. We have a soulful life to live, complete with a contract to fulfill. Our old lives are left in the ashes. Our new lives have taken flight. We have found our first set of spiritual riches.

Our NIRVANA has always lived within us. Our rebirthing has validated this truth. There has been a release of all the emotional rags that have kept us from the lives we are here to discover. It would be good to affirm that even when it looks like your life is a disaster, it is never OVER. So, for those of us, who want to make quantum leaps, we will. For those of us, who do not, we won't judge, even if you choose not to take quantum leaps. Our guides and loved ones are waiting to be asked to guide us, if we choose to be ready.

A Higher Power is on a positive high watch from the time we hit our emotional bottoms to the time we ask for help. We have never been alone. We just have not been aware of the help circling us. There is not a right or wrong time under universal law. The right time is whenever the decision is made. It is not possible to be in a place where we are ready. *Why?* Well, because our souls are still learning and still preparing. Whichever way we choose to go, it will still be considered positive. We will receive the positive results that we have chosen to experience.

There will come a very positive time and day of manifestation for the good or bad people we are live with. It is time to move forward towards our greater good. And, interestingly enough, our greater good may be in the form of a lesson that teaches us that we need to succeed in our quests for spiritual riches. Substance abuse, in all forms, will no longer take the pain away. In addition, alcohol, prescription drugs, sex, food, or whatever, will work for us until we find a bigger than life brick wall. *The course has been run.*

The time spent in the escape of addiction is over. It no longer takes away the pain of our past, present and future fears. This temporary fix has become just that - positively temporary. Opportunities are now upon us to change, to change our thinking patterns. And, when that occurs, many of us will have changed just one thing. *Everything.* There are those that say, "I do not have an addiction. I just need to calm down. I will change what I use to something less addictive." But, in addiction, anything that is mind-altering can get out-of-control.

Therefore, it is good for us to understand that many of us are addicted to something. If we pick the right and healthy addictions, it will be in our best interests. We will find that our addictive goods, in a certain area of our expertise, is beneficial to all. When switching addictions, we can find something that is much more self-serving than mind-alternating drugs. The goal is to use those passions to act out our addictive natures.

Everyone has a point of surrender, so that they become the best that they can be. Hard as it is for some, and easier for others, everyone in this lifetime learns how to surrender to someone, or something. Once we have tapped into our higher conscious selves, we become "teachable" to why surrender is such a powerful tool. Surrender affirms lives that not only bring the promises of spiritual richness, but also the success living within us. Our emotional rags have brought us a long way at this point. We are beginning to fully understand.

With eventual certainty we all succumb to our own self-induced overdoses. It seems a necessary process in our life cycles to find out what works, and what does not. We live with the "yin and yang," the ups and downs, and many opportunities that are not just by chance, to access our greater higher selves. Brought to our knees of total realization, we finally understand why we are so sick of being sick and tired. Some will say ... a bell goes off. A light goes on. A click in our consciousness snaps us into a foggy reality that we will never forget. Any addiction is silently promised a wakeup call to heal... Always! Caught in the moment of truth, and there is no escape for any form of addiction.

Exposed, and in the light of truth, addiction ends up begging to be healed. When the time is up, the time is up! Hiding is no longer an option. It no longer works. The spiritual richness that shows up is lights of opportunities for us to ask, listen, and learn the answers delivered through the spiritual energies that have been waiting to bring us into a new way of thinking and living. Help is always on the way, when we are on our way!

Emotions can run rapid, because egos hate giving up control. *Many ask, now what? What's next?* Suicidal thoughts fueled by the ego can add to confusion. The powerful minds of egos are not related to a life of mindfulness - listening and receiving. Egos want to direct a soul's addictive journey with thoughts. But the soul fired our egos, and, as a result, has found that a life free of addictive thinking and behaviors is a much softer, easier way. Yes, there is life to live, on life's terms, bridges to cross, miles to run, and mountains to climb. But, now we are able to engage in all that life provides for us. And, a quiet nudge reminds us that if we listen, we will have all the hope and trust, we need to get through anything. There is hope in all of us. It is the best survival technique, we could ever want. Hope keeps us going, when nothing else feels or looks like it will. An emotional rag may allude to mentally incapability of not having the power to move.

It may also champion necessary changes. Interventions can save a life, but not "fix" an addiction. An addiction is truly a personal journey into change. A person, willing, can only address it and ready to face the demons of his or her ego, which has taken away their life.

In retrospect, an intervention is not a "for sure fix," but it helps the soul find a safe place, where it can receive the guidance needed, as it starts recovers from the addiction. It helps that individual own the life he or she is here to live. It takes the riches of the mind, body, and spirit and replaces "worn out" thinking patterns.

It may be a start for them, or it may be a beginning that gets revisited at a later date. The seed has been planted, and growth will follow, in the way it is nourished with good orderly direction, also referred to as GOD growth.

I have had many emotional rags of my own, and on a personal note, I will share with you a story about my dad. My dad was unable to admit that he needed help. During the middle and end of his life, he was spiritually bankrupt. He had lost his self-esteem, and replaced it with alcohol and prescription drugs. His family would not support him, or admit he needed help. They considered his mental illness and addiction a black mark on the family name. Fortunately, that kind of thinking has changed. We now help those with addiction and mental health issues. During the end of my father's life, he committed suicide by jumping off a 13-story building. The end of his life was sad, lonely, and spent in a local neighborhood bar, while his bar-mates listened to his stories of woe. How his family had brought him down. He was always alone. He was never able to fall back on himself, although he tried to find his Higher Power. Unfortunately, his judgment, anger, and fear kept him from a waiting loving spirit that would have helped him, if he could have surrendered. Two bartenders, three barstool buddies, and immediate family members, were in attendance at my dad's memorial service.

I am comforted, however, to have had contact with him, and to have felt his presence on a few occasions. I know he is healing. When he has come to me, it has usually been when I am feeling a loss. He does not stay for long, and he still comes through as a beaten soul, but better than he was. I can feel his empathy, his pain, and his willingness to heal whatever took him to addiction, and then to mental illness. His amends have been made and recognized.

And, when I talk about him, I share the brilliance of whom he really was. He had a great deal to offer, and was very creative, both in song writing and poetry. There is no longer a need to talk about what happened to me in my childhood, unless it is to help another person in a similar situation. I trust that my dad is being prepared to re-enter for a lifetime that will address the demons that took his life in this lifetime.

My dad's inability to address his sickness was the cause of his demise. It is comforting to think that the mental health community could have helped him, but he was never ready. He was never wrong. He was always right. And, because he was unable to be an authentic transparent person, he died a horrific death. If my father had been able to surrender, he would have been able to heal. His positive pushback to life eluded any spiritual riches that he may have enjoyed. So, this is a story about a soul that was perfect and whole, and had to die to find that out. Thank God we get to heal, and return to life as a spiritual warrior, and not a victim of our own self-made circumstances.

There are those, who "cry wolf" constantly referring to suicidal thoughts in order to gain recognition of their cries for help. But, as with any person beginning to heal, the poor ME's are more drama than truth. However, a trained doctor can assess this trauma, and validate the person's cry for help.

A Spiritual Richness that is understood in the mind of God, of which we are all part, follows the Emotional Rag to this delicate subject. God IS. We ARE connected to the God that is everywhere. This energy knows nothing about boundaries. However, when the ego has its grip, the mind of God eludes us and is not present until we come to out of a deep sleep.

My own personal grief could only determine in the end that my father had nowhere else to go. He was totally emotionally and spiritually bankrupt. He had sat in a bar for years. He had decided that a family that he himself had abandoned years ago abandoned him. He had lost his will to live, and his body would not die on its own even though he was racked with emphysema and barely able to breathe. Who knows what one is thinking when taking their own life? Was it a brave but rather brutal step? Do these deeply wounded souls check out of their pain to hurt themselves or others? These questions are not answerable...yet. But their cross over, brutal and sometimes violent, is a call to heal on the other side. A loving God, not accessed for healing in this life, is immediate to them in the next. Their guides and loved ones who had gone on previously are there to be the whom of compassion. And they are much better equipped on the other side to hold only love and not let judgment stand in the way of what is now a new classroom to heal the troubled soul. It has been intuitively given to me in a clear message that my Dad is learning many things and has been in various classrooms ever since he arrived on the other side. I recently was visited by him and felt his presence and the message he sent regarding the loss of my nine year old Airedale. Goldie had a stroke after a severe thunderstorm. Her transition was not expected. I was heartbroken, and my father let me know he was feeling my pain. I was grateful for his brief visit.

In saving out souls in our SOS mode we have to surrender to willingness to do the next right thing. And in that willingness to change, no matter what the change needs to be, we simply have to be willing to be willing. Inside each of us lives the truth. The reason we fail to see some things is not because we do not have them. We have it all. We are just lacking, in a moment of insanity, the ability to see our God within.

We may call our Source and Supply God, Buddha, Christ, a mountain or anything that speaks to a loving presence bigger than our own life that inspires us to change. A power greater than ourselves that wants us to have the power we need in this lifetime. It does matter what we call this energy bigger than ourselves. We were born into this lifetime to recognize and know that we have something bigger to guide us, listen to us and show up the minute we show up for further information on this thing called life. Self-care at this point is essential to being ready able and willing to be willing. First and foremost is simply finding something that will tell us that we love ourselves enough to change. The help appears just for the asking. Sound unreal? Too hokey? Too out there? How bad will we have to hurt to start getting just a sense that this is true? The determination can be made after we get brave enough, trusting enough and usually hurting enough to put our hands to our head and ask...sometimes beg... for a change. At this simple point the healing has begun. By asking a Higher Power that we are finally willing to recognize for help, we will be immediately supported. The Spiritual Riches will pour over us in books, people, places, and intuitive new thought. Loving support will come in the way we are in sync with a NOW moment and answers will come falling around us like the warmth of a wool overcoat in the middle of a sub-zero icy winter. We are loved until we can love ourselves. Interestingly enough we will somehow realize that even up until now, we have been cared for and kept safe. At that point with self-love and the support from others, our way becomes defined and revealed. We are on our way out of Emotional Rags to Spiritual Riches.

No one else can do our work. The work we need to do is ours and ours alone. This is a custom job and ours alone to walk through. But is it really work? It may feel like work to finally start thinking and doing what we need to do, but we will find after a while that we were working harder at not changing the way we were thinking. The downhill spiral of whatever we need to change suddenly does not look so impossible. That stopping point could be referred to hitting our bottom. And yet, there are always bigger bottoms to hit until we finally die of exhaustion. Those who need the wake-up call are at full attention.

Deep in our consciousness, a still small voice of hope will continue to gently remind us that there is something bigger than ourselves and that help is available just for the asking. Intuitively we will know that we are being lead out of the despair of Emotional Rags to a wealth of safety in the Spiritual Riches that lie ahead. So, how complicated is all of this and when will we get our Riches? There is only one major requirement. LISTEN, and do the next right thing as it appears in your heart and your head. The heart is now directing the head.

How can someone feel so low and still hear that small still voice that is calling out to us as we wait for our answers? How can we listen when we are still stuck in our own muck? We start by trying. We start by practicing. We become willing to meditate instead of medicate. It becomes time to change our thinking. We know it...and when we do, the old ways of hiding and disguising our feelings do not work anymore. Our temporary fix is no longer working.

The time comes when our guides and angels nudge us, along with our Higher Power. We have never been alone, and by showing up to a new way of thinking and living, we will know that we know that we know.

Time IS and is always on our side. We are never in the wrong moment, but we may be in the wrong awareness or lack thereof. With trust, there is a deep knowing that there is a way to find our answers. And trusting is the way we show ourselves and the God of our understanding that we too are doing our part. As we recognize that we are one with the God of our understanding, there is a trust that God will help those of us who are ready and that God must trust us enough that we will come to the point of being ready.

As the planets move in perfect synchronicity, we too join in the perfect timing of the Universe. When we are out of our own orbit, we will be unable to move freely and experience the magnificence that we are born into. However, at the moment of realization and of showing up to the ONENESS that we has always been available to us, we will be back in orbit circling the Universe with creative positive energy. The time comes. The time will be right. The moment of truth shines through and any emotional rag that we have so attentively been attached to is at risk of being annihilated with a Spiritual Richness of accepting our Higher Self for our direction and answers. It may be that we thought we would never ever be okay, that we would never have a chance for peace and that Spiritual Riches would elude us. We may have thought we were not good enough or healthy enough or that our hair had to be blonde. Whatever we were thinking in this way was just one more Emotional Rag ambushing our ability to experience Spiritual Riches. No one, no one is ever left out once they have surrendered to a change in thinking. The faith and the trust in the process… is our beginning. Up until now, for many of us, listening was one of our options. We knew it all and if we didn't, we believed we did and faked it. Rolling around aimlessly was not longer viable. We were called on our shit, and it was time to change. If the time is right and we are really ready to make the commitment to allow change to bring us to our senses, it will happen. We will finally not only want to change but we will *become* the change.

Not all of us have to have the requirement of hitting a horrific emotional bottom. Many of us do not have to lose everything to get our attention. But those of us with High Bottoms will face another ego dilemma. The Ego will love telling us that we are not that bad. We really do not have to change that much. We are not like the rest of the world who are changing their thinking to change their lives. But the common denominator for all change is that everyone must do one thing, no exceptions. That one thing is to change one thing…EVERYTHING. It sounds like a tall order, but those of us who have changed everything have realized what that means. A change in thinking automatically changes everything. It may take some time, but it will happen as we change our thinking. Those of us who still are not willing…We will be the ones that insist on doing most everything the same old way, think the same old thoughts, and keep showing up to the same old things. And we are the ones that will continue to get the same old results. Yet again we will be right on time. We are not ready yet. The success of changing our thinking will by-pass us, and our ego will keep us afloat until we are faced with the next crisis.

In a world of Spiritual Riches, Change does occur. It just cannot help it. It has to. That is a principle that was coined by Earnest Homes, Science of Mind called the Law of Cause and Effect. What we think is what we get. What we do is where we are. How we live is what is in front of us. We are the cause that produces the effect.

Fortunately, there are many who do not need to totally bottom out before the Universe steps. High Bottoms of change do not lose it all. There is no need to lose it all. But this does not discount the fact that there is willingness and commitment needed and work to be done. The work is the catalyst to receiving the Spiritual Riches. The rags are changed out for a for a brand new cashmere coat life style. It is warm, abundant and been waiting for all of us. The work begins to search for the road to Spiritual riches. It is out there, and at this point of willingness we seem to know it.

Some of us tend to be more present and have received our wakeup call without the loss of health, family, and personal processions. We can be thankful that we did not experience a bottoming out where we lost everything...yet.

Life is really never lost. We may be lost, but we can return to life at any point in time that we are willing to make a commitment and choice. In the grand scheme of things, we are here to live our lives and have all that we need.

The Universe only knows positives. We do not have a doubting Thomas for a God. We do, however, have the opportunity to co-create. This becomes a positive life with the positive God of our understanding. But we are called upon to change the way we think.

We are cause, and effect follows. Our living is always Cause... creating results, the Effect, and what we do and how we think is always going to be under the Law of Cause and Effect.

We eventually come to realize that we are ONE with the Universe and with the God of our understanding. We finally come to believe that we are developing a personal relationship of co-creation with the God of our understanding and we are doing it in the Now. If we remain separate and not available to this ONENESS Principle, our lessons are many and full of egotistic mind chatter. The ego loves to take us out of our peace. But if we live a life in surrendering to what is, the ego is powerless. ONENESS becomes obvious as we face the adversity that shows us opportunity and we are not in control. We are part of a process of co-creating, but we are no longer separate from the God of our understanding. The wakeup call is magical and soon leaves the miracle status to a normal everyday status of having the Riches of ONENESS by knowing the Universe and its perfect synchronicity. We are all lined up just as the planets orbit, so do we? Yes we have a comfortable orbit when we stay in our NOW. When we are out of sync, we are out of our orbit. The only way back is to count on the Source that gave us the orbit in the first place. And this gives us back our NOW: the gift of the present moment.

We all have the opportunity to have the life we are here to live. And in every life there are a wakeup calls. We get to experience the legend of the PHOENIX. The Phoenix legend is one of adventure, lessons, and rebirth. Rebirthing can happen many times in the current lifetime we are in. When we have the experience of surrender, along with lessons in truth, we are reborn once we change the way we are thinking and move into a more synchronized orbit with the Universe. Each time we are reborn, we find a better life waiting for us. We took the time. We put in the time. We learned a new way of thinking and living and have realized a life with many gifts to bestow upon us. And with lessons realized we again are in opportunity to be reborn and move into our next incarnation. This is an incarnation that has more fulfillments. We are working our way to engaging in our sacred contract. The process takes what it takes to get there. As we show up to our life, our life shows up to us. We can do that many times in a life time or not. It is always an independent decision, and it is up to us. Choice will always be the game changer.

We will find life to be full of Spiritual Riches once we are committed to seeking out the formula and road map that leads the way. We are the ones who attract the gifts that we are here to receive. And when we come to know that no one else can do it for us, we have stumbled on a major milestone in the process of self-healing. We are not only experiencing a miracle but we become a miracle. To expect a miracle is to claim the miracle that we already are. That is what a real miracle truly is!

By affirming our lives by the gathering of new information, our dreams become reality. Our life begins to be lived in the present moment with a future jump started and created by living in the NOW.

Our dreams are realized to be more than frivolous daydreams. We can finally show up to the life we were born to live. Those of us who know that abundance is much more than the lottery is fortunate. And for those that are still not aware of what total abundance means, it becomes apparent at a point when money is not enough to bring us the peace and happiness we are seeking.

The next few chapters are easy. They are direct and to the point with no jibber jab. We are going to share some examples in a new way of thinking. Actually this new way of thinking is very old, but all was lost in fearful fundamental practices. These practices do serve their purpose for a time. But when a soul is ready to grow, a direct connection to the Universe is needed. We begin to want a personal relationship with the God of our understanding.

BLUE COLLAR SPIRITUALITY is much of the subject that we will be learning about. Simplistic in nature, this simple way of living is hard to adapt to because of all the past thinking. We have been taught that we must work extra hard to get what we want and need. However, it may be found that a simple approach to Universal Law is work enough without making it harder.

A solid work ethic in our spiritual life works just like it does in our secular life. We are rewarded by attending to the business of who we are. We show up every day, and everyday shows up to us. We benefit by the showing up process if we are willing to listen and hear what the next right thing to do is.

In learning this new principle, the only place to begin is at the beginning. But is this not true for everything we want to accomplish? There may be some varied experiences that may not fit for some and do fit for others. However, it will all be related. Take what you need and leave the rest. We are in this together, and we will get there once we drop separation and wear the Universal Coat of Oneness. No one is graded. There is no dunce hat or punishing corner to sit in until we get it.

A Personal Rags to Riches Story: I was so caught in a web of dysfunction growing up: A mentally challenged father who today would have been diagnosed with multiple disorders, a mother who I dearly loved but was a victim to a marriage that was abusive and not at all working, and then there was me, muddling through the depression, insecurity and feeling of constant abandonment. Terrorized by my father verbally, sexually, and physically, I remember sitting on the front steps our home on a street called Shangrai La Drive thinking about when I could leave. I was five years old. I was full of emotional rags that hurt to a point that I had no life. My brother, sister and I were not allowed to leave the property. There were no bikes. No after school activities and no Christmas or birthdays. No, there was only the word no you cannot and no you won't and if you do…major consequences. The children at school, the neighbors, and even some of my mother's relatives were thought to be of the world and we were not to associate with them. Even though Catholics flanked us on each side of the homes, my father took it upon himself to judge them because of their religion. Our home was filled with anger, fighting and yelling out four letter words and accusations about my mother and her being a whore. Nights were tough, especially when my father came home drunk and had my mother crying more than usual and we children were forced to cry along with her as the abuse continued into the wee hours of the morning. These are what I call Emotional Rags. The Riches were hard to realize at such a young age. But there was one Rich thing that happened everyday…my father left to go to work and was gone for a few hours. Granted, the energy still stayed gray in the home. But what a relief to have the Riches of him being gone. As I got older, I started getting more involved in the Kingdom Hall of Jehovah's Witnesses by doing the magazine placement and attending five meetings a week. This was another form of Riches. I was out of the house. But as I grew older and more present to the truth about myself, the Emotional Rags set again. I found myself feeling that the Witnesses were a cult and on the wrong track. Or maybe I felt I was on the wrong track and the Witnesses would find me out. They did. They did because of an affair, short lived that I had with a gal at work. I was about 17. My mother found out as the girl told me she was pregnant. This was untrue. But to save my mother from dying in God's War, Armageddon, I had to confess to a committee at the Kingdom Hall. I did and it was truly an Emotional Rag. But the Riches came soon after the grueling meeting I had to sit through. Many intimate questions were asked. I was judged. I was exonerated with conditions. I did not like the conditions and never went back. I had not been dis-fellowshipped from that organization by a committee of men. No, I took that on disfellowshipped and myself myself that fateful day. That was a day of freedom and Riches. That was the day the Lord had made! LOL

Chapter Two

The Soul's Journey of Re-entry= OUCH!

WE ARE BORN. FOR MANY of us this is not our first time around. We may want it to be because with a new life comes the responsibility to clean up the past so that we can move on to a higher level of consciousness. We all come in with unexplained gifts and talents that will manifest the creative soul we are. Rebirthing is a natural and normal way in nature. We too are part of the reincarnation process. Dying is not an option, and living is what we are here to do. We may die to a life we have, but we will always be reborn to a new life with an opportunity for a new beginning. This helpful realization aids us in making sense of our lives and leaving fear out of the equation.

We have been with our parents and family members before in many different roles. Because of our Oneness, we are continuing to learn together until we have come to a successful and loving closure. We will realize and understand that if we take a moment to go within and just feel the lessons and love we have for those that are closest to us. We are always in preparation for our next sacred contract.

As much as we may want to analyze past life experience, it really is of no use in the NOW. It is good to know that we are here to finish what we started. Any nudge we receive from our past to help us complete this lifetime is always a welcome plus. But in the end, we are here do our work so we can go on to the next incarnation experience. Emotional Rags are all a part of this process.

This does not sound very conventional, especially if we were brought up in a fundamentalist religion. But having an open mind and staying open to all possibilities will give you any and all information you are now ready to receive. A new way of knowing can take you to a new place of living. By allowing ourselves to show up to some new thought, we become available to at least consider our options. And if there is a formula that is working at this time, it is the answer presently until that formula no longer works. Our formulas constantly change as we change to become better at who we are. So in the next few chapters, take what you can use and leave the rest.

We all get to customize our journey and develop that special personal relationship with the Universe: the God of our understanding that is and has always been in our NOW. Our emotional rags have answers. So showing up to new thought and giving your life a chance at having it all will surely prove to be worth the effort. That effort once learned will become invaluable and effortless. More will be revealed in the coming chapters about how we become effortless.

Being born is one thing. Showing up is another. But as always, we have the choice. We had the choice in other lifetimes and we have the choice now. If we do not choose to grow and change, we will always get another chance. We are not judged but waited for. The extravagant love that we are seeking is the extravagant love that lives within us. We are connected to it at all times, but the rags get in our way. Once we intuitively know that we have a kind and loving God, our biggest emotional rag is gone. Once we know that the Universe works in our best interest, one more emotional rag disappears. In a moment of sanity and simplicity, we realize that we have a chance to align with the planets and the stars and if we do…we are freely given the tools to complete what we have come to do.

So the emotional rags are yet another way of saying, "You are living in the field of total opportunity and as you grow into your ONENESS you will be amazed before you are halfway through." And as always and with anything and everything, the best way to start is at our beginning. The beginning is where we first started collecting emotional rags. It is good to take a glimpse at early life. Do not dwell on it, but look to see what is holding us back. What is that keeps surfacing and effecting how we live and how we think? What happened, what was going on, and did we feel that we had a good start or are we still blaming our parents? Were they here to learn and grow too? How did they do? Did they grow and find their way? What we felt we were and are dealing with are most likely the same things their background challenged them with. The question can be poised in this way: What caused them to raise us in a way that left us with our current lessons?

And are we ready to put a halt to this on-going lesson that keeps affecting generation after generation? How seldom we think of what they were learning. How often we want to blame them for what we think they did not learn. In doing so, our families take the heat of multi- generational emotional rags. Is this finally the opportunity to release what we think has been done to us? Or did they do it for us? What can we now do to grow, and are we the ones called to put a halt to all that insanity? Are we the ones who get to heal not only ourselves but also a whole family by not continuing on with generations of emotional rags? Yes, we do get this opportunity. But are we willing to address the NOW of our lives, change the energy, forgive and let go and then move on? Spiritual Riches are surely awaiting our return to sanity.

Let's see what it takes to partake of the gift of Oneness and have it all. We all have our stories, and here is one of mine. I share this with you because I have healed the wounds that were binding me. And this is the authentic and transparent account of a family of birth and its lessons of opportunity. I choose to grow.

So a personal example of early life for me looks like this: I remember being a young boy of four or five, sitting on some bare concrete front steps in my home holding my head and asking myself…"When do I get to get out of here?" I was depressed and lonely and full of abandonment in a household filled with horrors of many lessons. My father was mentally ill and not admitting that he needed help. My mother was not admitting that he needed help and was trying to keep the relationship going. That's what wives were told to do in the 1950s.

The screaming, bickering and fights centered on fear, jealousy, religion, and blaming anyone and everyone except the perpetrator throwing out this negative energy. That was my father. This was a common everyday occurrence. My mother cried often. My brother was constantly in trouble and started obsessively masturbating at an early age. My sister kept getting up in the middle of the night and taking everything out of her room to obsessively clean and then put everything back. The neighbors heard the screaming and yelling. I was living in fear of what my father would say and do and constantly felt embarrassed by him. I was always on the alert for abuse and I always felt that I must protect my mother. This separated me from my siblings. And I wanted some sort of recognition from my father but only got it when I was forced to watch him bathe while he made me recite the 23rd Psalm. And then I would watch him rubbing himself inappropriately in front of me either at the sink or in the tub. My brother went through some of this too.

However my memories of childhood are no longer my emotional rags. What did I do? Who did I forgive? What was the freeing moment that allowed me to learn the lessons around this behavior so that I will never have to go there again? It took some time but I got there. Here is what worked for me until I totally surrendered. Then I started to heal.

Nothing worked for a few years. I was trapped in that hellhole of a house for 16 years. I left. I finished high school and as I made my way to a new life, I was still filled with fears. I wanted change. I needed help. And to my surprise there were people out of the blue showing up to help me. One was my high school girlfriend's father. He took me in. He made me laugh. He let me live in his home with his family. I was amazed at the love this home and the family that lived there offered in comparison to what I had come from. This man put me to work and signed for my first car. I was in awe and so grateful.

Then this man I respected and loved started drinking, left his wife, and abandoned his family and me for a younger woman. His life became a life of crime when he began stealing from the company where he worked. I was saddened but still to this day love him for what his real soulful self did to me. I learned later that he was an alcoholic who had stopped drinking but returned to his insanity for reasons that are unknown to me. In all truth I now realize his lessons with alcohol were not over...yet.

I was again on my own. I decided to get married to a girl I had been dating. I was told intuitively not to marry, but I was not good at listening. My fear was that if I did not marry her, I would never marry. To never marry was my guides and angels' nudge to me letting me know that marrying a woman was not my journey for this lifetime. I married and realized finally that I was a gay man. So I divorced. I hurt the girl I had married deeply. After we married I found that I loved her so much that I had to let her go and not live a double life.

My Jehovah's Witness days were well over. I no longer associated with them as my upbringing had included their doctrine. No Christmas, birthdays, holidays, blood transfusions, saluting the flag, military service or association with anyone that was not a Witness. They also did not believe in Halloween. I guess they did not like people showing up to their door.

Growing up, my father had a tight control on the family by making us abide by the rules of what I now consider a cult. The people were good but were controlled by fear.

My twenties came, and I found myself angry with God. I had only known fear from my family and the religion I had been brought up in. I never really succumbed to this unhealthy religion in the end. My intuitive sense had matured and was giving me other messages. I found myself wanting to know the truth about this thing called God, but it took some time away to be able to come back for the answers.

I started to hide behind alcohol, which was my medication for a few years. I got into the swing of life and became a liar and totally hidden from who I was. The drinking helped...for a while. Finally I started asking out loud for information on the Universe and a Higher Power that could help me. The books came from everywhere and I was drinking up information that sounded so familiar and made so much sense.

A personal story of Emotional Rags to Spiritual Riches

Before I even had a chance of detoxing from alcohol I had to detox from family, religion, and my un-authentic self. The Emotional Rags that started to pile up were huge. My life was over-run with emotion, health issues, job issues, and an inability to function properly in a normal 24hr day. I was hiding from everything, and my drinking hit a new high. I had finally crossed the line, and I knew it. I remember saying just before this happened, why I can't feel this good all the time. I loved the high. I loved not remembering. I sedated myself until my problems were blacked out of my mind. It was my Nirvana. It was Riches every time it happened, and it happened every day. But there came that fateful day when I realized that I could not stop drinking. I was now in yet another set of Emotional Rags that were coming around me. I fought it. I did not want to let go of the way I found my peace. And the sickness set in. The hangovers were horrendous, and I was starting to drink in the morning so that I could get rid of the pain. The pain just got worse. I started missing work. I was not paying my bills. I became deeply sad for the first time using a substance. I was in Seattle, Washington on a project job and on my 40th birthday, I received a new set of Riches. I landed in a 28-day treatment program for alcoholism. It was the beginning of the end...but it took what it took in the months and years ahead to change one thing...EVERYTING. My Emotional Rags had turned to Riches, but it sure did not feel like that was what was happening to me. I was totally unaware of the real world and I was being forced to start over. Thank God!

Chapter Three

ALCOHOL TOOK OVER UNTIL I was 40. I hit my bottom and lost everything. I knew I had a problem but was unwilling to address it. So the Universe addressed it for me. At 40 I died. My old life was gone and my new life was to begin. I was having a breached re-birth, and it hurt like hell. But without the slam and slap to the ground, I would have died early in this life, missing my mark. I had much to do and much to learn and so I started the healing that was so needed to give myself the life that I wanted. We all know intuitively that we are here for the greater good. But until we become the Greater Good, it really does not matter.

There I was…in AA, going to three meetings a day, seven days a week and holding on to my ass. Why me??? Had not I had enough pain. NO! It's over when it's over and we start to get it! So one day at a time was how I first realized the NOW of my soul's journey. I was a hole in a doughnut. Somewhere along to way I had been living in emotional rags. The hiding, the lying, along with no transparency had taken its toll. I was down for the count. Thank God! So I was one of those people who had to hit an uncomfortable bottom. For me it was alcohol, but for others it can be many things. Addiction knows no boundaries except to keep feeding the ego with bad information. Obsessive compulsive thinking for those of us who do not know how to heal addiction becomes a choice of the ego. I personally am grateful for addiction stepping in. I did not die. I was forced at the end, when my addiction was no longer working, to move into a changed thought system or die. Your story may be different. It may be harder. It may be a lighter life sentence…but it is your story and it is where your healing can begin once you surrender. Many times we get taken to the limits before the light goes on and we have nowhere else to go. Addiction of any kind is the cancer of the soul that wants to heal whatever needs healing. The Emotional Rag was being so sick and the Riches that had to be learned by JUST SHOWING UP was the process it would take. LETTING GO...NO REALLY! REALLY LETTING GO! It sounds easy to say it, but it was one of the hardest things we as humans have to learn.

Many of us are very competent at listening to our ego tell us that we can surrender and we can let go. Why many of us have done it 150 times. However, in the chatter of our monkey mind, we are still conjuring whatever it takes in a fearful mode to revisit the past and predict the future. Who could even hope to let go with all that sabotaging going on? Our past and future thinking is all old news that we continue to carry with us on our own front page of life. We may want to let go, and some of us even put it in the editorial section to see if anyone is watching of reading our failed attempts. Then comes a day when we are so exhausted trying to do all this change and surrender on our own, that we think it may be wise to give something bigger than ourselves yet another try.

This time we are too tired to keep taking our scattered chaotic Emotional Rags back. And maybe, just maybe, we have reached our breaking point of letting go and letting God. But even worn down, the ego may go on some temporary oxygen and try to revive us back to full control. Again. Like my mother, who never surrendered, always said - when a problem arose, "Pull UP your bootstraps and get going!" She had been told that as a girl growing up. But those boots were a bad fit for her. If she had surrendered in her adult life, she could have avoided 23 years of abuse before she finally took the plunge. And she was not wearing any boots. She jumped into the abyss of a restraining order on my abusive father and later divorced him. But she had finally gained her power through the act of surrender. She had help from a God of her understanding and her guides and loved ones. At first she was scared and then she got scared of being sacred. Surrender was her only option left. Years later she would look back and remember that fearful yet important decisive day. She was looking back after another marriage that was not abusive and one where she got to experience some good healthy times.

The Emotional Rags my mother dealt with and then healed were a direct result of her childhood. She was not treated well all through her year of growing up. Her stepmother was ruthless, jealous, and herself wounded. Right up until the death of my Grandmother she was still dishonoring my mother. One now gets to question where her wounded soul had been. But with surrender my mother finally healed old wounds, found her self-esteem, and lived out her life reasonably content.

She got the opportunity to surrender her Emotional Rags and then found her Spiritual Riches. And now her own children would have that opportunity as well. We had watched the surrender and the healing and were educated by example as to how and when and why to surrender. In the Now of our lives, the Emotional Past had happened. And healing became the hallmark of showing up to be able to finally let go. It works if we work it.

Chapter Four

MANY EXPERIENCES IN OUR LIFE are filled with hurt, fear, and abandonment. But coming to realize to that our own Emotional Rags of hurt, fear, and abandonment are the gateway to opportunity may be a new and different way to think. Opportunity comes to many of us in many strange unintended ways. My mother and her Emotional Rags that needed healing were right in front of her as they are in all us. I championed her efforts and in the end she championed mine. She did the best she could at the time and all the time right up until she surrendered. Most of us do. Years later we would have a conversation in which she revealed to me that she wished she could have been better, done better. How often many of us feel this way. But the truth is, that as for my mother and for all of us, it takes what it takes to get us where we need to go. That is the reality of what surrender really looks like. In the letting go process, what is the right way and what is the wrong way? Are we all no better and more compassionate because of all these Emotional Rags? And the conclusion to this question is yes we are, once we have walked our talk and surrendered to the Rags that have been holding us back from the revelation of our true soul. We do survive the process as uncomfortable as it may be. We do finally let go. We let God. We are finally free. When all is said and done, we come to understand that it is easier to heal than not to heal. The experience of healing our Rags promotes a quick turn-around on any new ones that may try to infiltrate our life.

A personal story Emotional Rags to Spiritual Riches

My mother. My mom. My lovely sweet mother had an early life with a stepmother that was hell for her and her brother. Her pick of men were not great but full of lessons on building self-esteem, being independent, and becoming fully who she really was. And she was something else. Everyone who knew her loved her, and she had a great deal of support from one friend in particular and my Aunt as to what she was dealing with in respect to my father. But her lessons were hard until she found her voice. It took 23 years of an unsuccessful marriage for her to move on. I was there through it all being her champion and helping in the best way I could by supporting her next right moves. She was moving out of fear and into freedom and at the time it was minute by minute. She had suffered years of Emotional Rags, and there was no one to fix her but herself. I thought I could fix her. That is what love does when it is inexperienced and needing to grow on its own, within its own. But nevertheless I did try and even though I protected, cared for, and watched over my mother, I never fixed her. She did a great job on her own. She remarried and it was a better marriage, but she was definitely the caretaker. She had re-gained her self-esteem and as always, gave the marriage her all. Any flaws of emotions left unhealed were sensed by her new husband and used to upset her. But she would recover quickly from these upsets. She had married a very emotionally young soul. But he was not mentally ill, and he did participate in the marriage to heal his own wounded experience from his first wife. It was all great lessons for both and it helped both of them. It helps to remind me that the Universe is always on time. We live. We learn. We grow. We move on. She moved on at 75 and is now in the bliss of what she would call her heaven. She visits me regularly and leaves quickly. She is supportive and has been with me in many lifetimes. Are we done? I am not sure, but I will be so happy to be with her for an extended length of time before I return to Planet Earth. That to me is Rich.

Chapter Five

Let's Stop Our Red Wining

THIS CHAPTER HAPPENS TO BE more on the Emotional Rags of addiction, but for those of us who have used any substance, including food, sex, or gambling to escape ourselves will understand the Emotional Rags of this continued story.

Personally speaking, red wine was my drug of choice and so was white and so was vodka and so was beer. I think we get the point... There was not a winery big enough to service my needs or so I thought. White wine was also my "whine" of choice and Mr. Fix it. And martinis with double olives, straight up in a classy crystal martini glass. "No ice" was a drug I used when I wanted to feel like a classy guy who knew how to medicate with style. I used to say about any drink served on the rocks that "It just gets in my way!" And yet I still called myself a social drinker. I must admit that at the time, alcohol was the medication that kept me from meditating. It was my unhealthy friend. It soothed my troubled soul and kept my ego active with justification. I was secretly troubled with my own Emotional Rags. What was there to address or admit when my best buddy understood? Alcohol was my buddy and definitely my drug of choice.

I never outwardly whined but I always took my buzz to the finish line and blocked out an entire lifetime in three hours to six hours or passed out, whichever came first. My whining was always painfully living inside me darkening my soul.

When I came to in the morning, everything was still blocked out as my hangovers were always brutal. Underneath the hangovers and the alcohol were a million or so emotional rags that my ego relentlessly would not let me forget. And in any kind of sober state, I would be reminded. I sometimes got a short reprieve in the mornings only because I had to manage the hangover.

And then the monkey mind would start the chatter and return my head to the Emotional Rags that were raging. But I had the fix. I would start the process of taking the Emotional Rags away with the medication that was legal and worked for me. My nectar of the Gods worked until it didn't work. That day came as the disease of alcoholism has a beginning, middle and an end. When the time came and I could no longer function, I was a 24/7 drinker, I somehow knew my time was up. My Emotional Rags could no longer be shut out with my drinking. They were harder to hide and in the end there was no real way to do so. I was caught in my own mess. Only this was one of the biggest Emotional Rag Messes I would ever have to address. It was the tip of my iceberg. I had so many emotional rags stuffed inside me that once the alcohol was gone, I was exposed... yes totally exposed to this thing called life. I was naked and venerable like never before.

Oh my God...it was time to either do one of two things. Keep drinking and die young or stop drinking and die old. Dying young meant taking with these Rags to another life and in all conscious sanity I could not imagine that as a choice I would take. I had been somewhat aware of a spiritual connection for a long time. I kept hearing that I had work to do. I never realized how much work it would take to dispel my demons.

My shame is gone. My Rags are gone. But until I came to know the truth about who I was and why I was doing what I was doing to hide my life, I could not heal. Everyone has something that wants to nudge them into healing. It can be anything from alcohol to any other addiction or wakeup call that it takes to help us meet ourselves in the light of truth. This is why I choose to share my story in the effort to relate and help others by giving them the hope that was given me. So to continue.

It becomes second nature to look for help to survive terrible emotional traumas and dramas. My family had the dis-ease of alcoholism and I was a perfect candidate to use this substance to hide the past 40 years of my life. I needed every drop until I dropped. It kept me sedated and shut down until I was ready to heal. Yes, I am one of those who wished I had gotten the memo sooner, but that was not me. I had to face my own music and was forced into front and center and the world was my audience. Yikes!

What was I to do? What was I going to do and how was I going to be able to even show up? I had to put one foot in front of the other and no matter what just keep showing up. I did, but my feet were dragging for a long time. I was so out of sync and everything and everybody looked foreign to me. Oh well. To heal is to stand emotionally naked and start asking for help. AA was my first stop, and it helped for years. I definitely have AA on the to-do list for anyone addicted to drugs and alcohol. Bill Wilson's 12 Step Program gave me my life back.

Addiction to alcohol is very common because it is legal. But it is not the quick fix most of us hoped for. The truth is that drugs and alcohol will just add another layer of emotional rags, just another layer to address and heal.

All and all, the family disease has little to do with addiction. It seems to be more correctly put that it is only a crutch to not change. It is a curse that is self-induced, but there is a way out if we are willing. Any one of us has the capability to stop the wounded family drama. It lives within us, and we can count on the help we need. We have to ask and then affirm that we already have Higher Conscious guidance, but we need to know how to access the key to opening the door to Spiritual Riches. Just acknowledging that we are finally aware of a way to dump our Emotional Rags in itself is an affirmation that will attract a life changing experience. We have accessed enlightenment.

A personal example of more Emotional Rags to Spiritual Riches around the topic of addiction:

It was a hard time to sober up. All the feelings I had felt were surfacing. And it was not only the recent predicament I was in; I was faced with feelings from childhood through my present adulthood that I had drunk away for years. My sexuality was staring me in the face square on, and I was not able to hide anymore. My feelings were on the outer layer of my skin. I felt totally exposed.

Spending 28 days in a treatment center in the state of Washington had been safe. I was sober when I left. I would rather say I was dry. My thoughts were not about sobriety. I wanted to drink but had all these flashes in my head of what I had learned about alcoholism. Why I drank, what the disease was all about, that I was in late stage with a damaged liver, and the shakes that made me start my morning drinking to get rid of the hangovers. Leaving the treatment center was scary. I was raw. Returning to work was scary. Living at all was scary. I was so out of a normal element for me. My life was now AA meetings, AA meetings, and more meetings. I went until about three months until someone said to me when I asked them why I felt so bad that it just gets worse. I drank and I drank until I was sedated. But this time I had too much information and it did not feel good or right. I got back on track and suffered through until I got a job offer in Sarasota, Florida. I went to market a company for a friend and co-worker of mine. I arrived and started drinking again as I would need to drink to entertain clients. My soggy brain informed me along with a very low self-esteem ego that this was the way to go. The job went okay until once again I perceived that the owner mentioned my sexuality over the phone. To this day I am not sure that happened. But it might as well have as I wrote a steaming letter and copied the world. It was a letter of resignation. My buddy alcohol duped me again. I have since made amends to this man. I love him. I love his family, and I wanted to do a great job getting his company started. But when beer started showing up in my bottom drawer, the job was over for me.

My best friend's mother and dad rescued me again. They loved me unconditionally and always said I would land on my feet. What a set of Emotional Rags I had to experience to land sitting straight up. I then moved in my best friend, and she was drinking and using some drugs at the time to lose weight along with some recreational drugs with her boyfriend. I was okay with that and just kept going to AA meetings. I took a housesitting job for another AA member who lost her mother and then went back to college. I was on a great track, had a great new friend helping me and felt very solid with the progress I made. I received a job offer from LA for a great deal of money. I was on my way after a year and a half of college and no drinking. I finally was well. I felt great. I felt so good that I decided I could drink again. I did. And eventually in LA the same thing happened to me that happened before. I was on my way to Louisiana for another contract job. I worked and drank from home. I did not work very much that year.

Then my job took me to Richmond, Virginia for a management job that I was not prepared for. I had a nervous breakdown after mixing pills and booze. I almost died. Did I stop drinking? No. I could not handle the Emotional Rag of coming off all that alcohol and pills. So I managed the disease the best I could. I needed another rescue, got it from home, moved back again and tried my best to sober up. But I could not get there. I was not able to stop...even with meetings...even with a sponsor. My disease was holding me hostage. I finally got another job offer in New Jersey. I showed up, went immediately to a bar, and ordered a glass of white wine. I was unable to drink it. Something had happened. I was getting an intervention from something bigger than myself.

After a few days, I showed up to an AA meeting. I felt totally withdrawn and guilty for not being able to stay sober. I met a man called Joe, who was older, and who actually knew the founder of Alcoholic Anonymous (AA), Bill W. We talked, I shared my story, and he felt my guilt. He said just one statement to me, "David, you are still loved. You are a good person. Pick up where you left off, and get on with it." That was 16 years ago. He was the biggest piece of gold, I had ever seen. He told me something that I desperately needed to hear. I thank God for Joe. The spirit gave me a nudge through Joe. I got involved, stayed sober, and have had an incredible run since then.

For some reason…my ego had to go through all that it did to get my attention. The fear, the doubt, the depression all played an important role in me waking up. Thank God, I did not stop trying to become sober. The God of my understanding had a plan for me, and that plan was love. Love the ONENESS that we all are. Teach it. Nudge it. Be it. Without the pain…I would have never sobered up. Without the help of others my chances of recovery would have been slim. My riches are recognized, even when I am experiencing emotional rags. It takes what it takes for all of us. Out of my own life, I have lost judgments and resentment, and most of all; I have lost my fearful nature. And, if any of those character defects raise their ugly heads, I have tools to help me move through these feelings, because they no longer have a place in my life. Today, I love teaching, nudging, and being all that I have learned. I finally arrived at my sacred contract, and it was worth every step.

Chapter Six

Families that Rag Together Are Not Together

MOST ALL OF US HAVE a certain love for our families. Therefore, we want to fix what we don't like. We think we can really love them, and they, in turn, will really love and understand us. We actually think we can change our families to be more acceptable to our own personal needs. If our family members would only listen to us! There is one thing we can be sure of, after our attempt at family counseling, and that is - they are not going to change for us. However, after several jump starts, there is the possibility that we must change. And, as we get healthier, we begin to realize that our jobs concern only us. Everyone is entitled to his or her own journeys. We are not fixers, but we are also not enablers. Why prolong our own journeys or the journeys of others by convincing them it is a temporary fix. Truthfully, in order to grow out of emotional rags; we need to address our own journeys. That is the path to enlightenment.

"Well you know..." can be a very scary start to a sentence. It is the start to someone ready to tell us what to do, what we should think, and why he or she knows the answers to our problems. You "should" is also an ambush of someone, who is unable to listen, as we answer, face our challenges and heal ourselves. People just do not hear us, and we definitely do not hear them. *No one is listening.*

While we are living in our own emotional rags, we cannot fix anyone. And, once we have found our ways, we find there is no need to fix anyone. We have let go of one more Emotional Rag. We, instead, find that we are wiser, and more connected, along with being an empathetic and caring listener. We never were or, may I say, "I never was..." There is way too much chatter in daily life to be able to listen carefully. When it comes to fixing ourselves, it takes a universe full of guides, angels, and a God of our understanding, who patiently places listening champions in our paths. Their help is all about support. That is what we finally learn.

One of the most common signs of someone, who is not prepared to be our champion, is someone, who is struggling to quiet their own mind. This person also has not found his or her way to connect with a higher consciousness. As we learn to live in an ONENESS principle, we heal and begin to understand that we all have a required journey to travel. The ego holds us hostage, until we start to feel the enlightenment given to us, in order to start the process of "letting go." *It does come.* We realize that the unhealthy ego does not have the answers. But, most importantly, we finally understand that no one's ego is going to "cure" ours. Anyone telling us what we should do, and what will happen, if we don't, only complicates our own healing processes. Friends and family are so busy monitoring our lives, and comparing our journeys that their own journeys are quite disheveled. In other words, their egoist interest in our lives is more about their own lives.

More specifically, trying to tell another unhealthy person, who would like the job of controlling our lives, turns into a major derailment in our relationships. Anger, fear, and resentment are the result of these train wrecks. True kinship can only come when both parties are on healing quests.

We cannot discount the fact that we absolutely need our champions for support. The safest and most helpful souls in our lives are the ones that listen, support, and make suggestions based on their own experiences. If we have these gifts in our lives, we are able to make headway in our own personal growth. We are also able to learn, by example, what really works in healthy supportive relationships.

These helpful souls share in our emotional rags, only as a support system to our best intentions. At the end of our listening period, a healthy listener emerges. He or she lets go and lets God. They have chosen to love us, until we can love ourselves. *What a gift?!* They are our earthly angels standing by until we see our own wings sprout.

We are connected to our families of birth for good reason. Our goal with emotional rags is to heal them, so that we can move on to our own next level of service to the universe. When we do, our spiritual riches appear.

Birth families are the hardest lessons we have. There is so much love, but it can be so convoluted with past experiences that it, sometimes, appears to be anything, but deep love. In the process of the Christ-like or Buddha-consciousness, we are called to a spiritual healing. *Everyone wins.* All family members are being asked to heal. Some will and some will not. This cannot be our focus, or our job to determine, if we are embracing our own healings. Concentration on ourselves, many times, heals family members in ways that are hidden from our views. We have come into these lives perfectly suited to "souls," from past lives. We, well as may, need to experience, and heal lifetimes of emotional rags. Fortunately, this is not a sentencing, but an opportunity.

We may not heal all of what we need to heal with our families, but it is better to look at progress, not perfection in this endeavor. *We have time. They have time.* Time is not the enemy. Just know that time is on our sides. We can take the gift of time in increments. And, with the healing performed in increments of time, we experience increments of peace. There will come a time, when we lovingly and attentively show up, and be healed. At that time, we will be able to totally "let it be." Moreover, we will intuitively know that we are complete by the peace that we are feeling. At that time we will have eliminated our own emotional rags. We are ready to embark on a higher road, a more useful and fulfilling earthly contract. We begin by just showing up to our next right thing. *We have earned our wings.*

So, families that "rag" together cannot stay together, especially when one has healed, but the other one has not. This is not a call to separate, but a realization that we cannot fix anyone. There comes a point, in which family members, who are not getting their ways, and have been emotionally hurt again, or feel abandonment, no longer want us present in their still egoist problem-solving ways. Letting them be, means letting them have their lessons, and remembering that what they do is really none of our businesses. We have moved on. Through an ONENESS, we are connected. But, in a healing principle, in order for continued growth on our parts, their energies will not work, or help us, as we continue to grow. It is best to love them so much that we let them be. We let them be without anger, hurt, or resentments. Loving someone means loving him or her in all circumstances. But, loving our families, without comment, to grow on their parts, is a love that is like no other. *They can be right, but we can choose to be peaceful.*

A Personal Story of Emotional Rags to Spiritual Riches

A birth family, extended family, close friends, comrades at work and/or people, in general, that are in close contact, cannot stay together, if they are "ragging" about each other. In other words, if the past cannot be left alone, as well as the future, family and friends will stay in the rags of emotion. Personally, I have tried to hold on tight to my family, my friends, and my loved ones here on earth, and have found that, as I grew spiritually, I was losing them. I have tried hard not to let that happen. But, in my own understanding of what I share, as BLUE COLLAR SPIRITUALITY, I know that trying to hold on to anything, simply does not work. The only emotional rags arose because I was afraid to let go, I was in fear of becoming lonely and being alone. But, I was already lonely and alone having them in my life. It became clear that I had to start developing a good solid relationship with myself and be authentic and transparent enough not to let anyone or anything compromise my newfound truth. I was being tolerated for my changes but not loved in a way that would support, who I was becoming. The people that had been with me were no longer were in my court. *I had changed.* I was no longer an emotional rag. I did not need saving. I was not willing to fix anyone anymore. I had never fixed anyone anyways. That was an illusion, as my family and friends were fixing themselves to the degree that they were comfortable. And, I knew that I was making them uncomfortable. They just could not champion all my changes.

There was a new dawn approaching, and I was meeting likeminded people wherever I went. *They got me.* They knew what I was feeling, and what I was talking about. They were having the same issues with their old birth families and friends.

But, how could I be so insensitive to let them go…I just could not. So, for a few years, I talked to them about the same old things, the same old past, and listened to their same old issues. *Why not?* I loved them. Interestingly, I was getting help from the God of my understanding. It was help for all of us. I never had to let anyone go. They let me go. Some just let me be. I was released from old conversations, and the past that was still their NOW. Today, my riches are around them NOW with new insight. I am there to only listen. My suggestions are of no value in my outdated friendships and family connections. I have tried hard for years to keep my family intact. I wanted to because I thought it was my job. In other words, I got transferred to a new job with benefits. *Me. What did that mean?* Then, it finally came to me that loving others extravagantly in the NOW meant living on purpose. I meant to ask for nothing in outcomes, and just keep showing up and supporting positive changes. In other words, not expecting others to understand me - that was a big bundle of riches.

I have to admit that it was definitely lonely, when they started dropping off like flies, I held on until they let me go. I somehow knew that was the best thing to do. Intuitively, I worked with spirit and my guides. The timing was not mine. My job was to keep showing up to love them, and just be there. However, in one instance, I had to let a family member go. I was not able to even listen anymore, and I kept hearing was that it was not my job to fix anyone. No judgments needed on my part, and no resentments were formed. But, in order to be open to my own life and the messaging that was trying to come through, I could not be clouded with someone, who had decided on the outcome of our relationship, without asking me. *It was not easy.* However, loving unconditionally sometimes means stepping aside, so that the one you love gets to have his or her journey, without interference from other family members. So, I returned and stayed present to the high watch to make sure I was connecting with my own journey, and not someone, who was still stuck. There were times when I found myself wanting to react and engage in a conversation that would clear the air and be helpful. But, when I tried, I was cut off with old news. I had lost the connection with my family member years ago. I just was not willing to give up and let it go. Someone can hold you hostage, and tell you that they love you, but when you realize they don't like you, it is okay to step out of the ring of fire, and into a cool pond, in order to take the sting away. This is another set of riches, in which emotional rags are replaced with knowledge. My emotional rags could only re-appear, if I allowed them to continue to judge me for what they thought I was thinking. Assumption can be very dangerous to a soul trying to heal. I chose not to react to those things, anymore. I wanted the riches. I had done the work, and did not want to go back to those emotional rags.

When you face God head on, there is no turning back. And, when you look at God, and see him in the face of your family and friends, you end up seeing only the "best of the best" - that, in itself, is so rich.

Today in an on-going state of a life of enlightenment, I find I love all of them, even more than I thought I was capable of, but I still look on, from afar, so that they can live their lives the way they want to. We are all getting the gift of lessons, and my lessons are not theirs, and theirs are not mine. That is yet another gift of feeling and being rich.

Chapter Seven

The Ego Is Powerful Only
With Our Permission

THE ONLY TIME WE WILL ever have power is when we are not under the jurisdiction of our egos. At first this may sound very strange, but by letting go and letting God, we become full of co-creative power. We all know about that chatter box, loud mouth person, who always has to have his or her say. You know, that person, who lives in our heads and will not shut up. The one, who says "I am always right!" And, then, there are those vying for the same position with their own chattering egos that wants to be "Mr. Right." Two egos going to battle is a great example of two egos stuck in the right and NOW willing to budge, and in the end, no one has won. *No one could.* Even if it feels like there is a victory, the war is not over, the battle will re-appear, and the ego will once again be in a face-off...with itself.

The power of the ego is a sly, and waits for an opening. All of the sudden, we are fearfully defending something that does not need defending; or letting this chatter box take over in our heads with a case in point, the egos are all laid out in perfection, sidestepping our truths. The words are partly true, the truth is somewhat conveyed in a manipulative manor, just to win the dual. But, there was no dual, until the egos got involved. Defensively we find ourselves defending what we did or did not do. We chatter fast, and do not let in a breath of truth. The egos are in full charge, or are they? We are in our ego's dramas. When egos think that they are in charge, we repeat the same conversations over and over again, until we bypass the pesky entity, and start shooting from the heart with transparency, authenticity, and a great deal of breathing. This breath is the key to bypassing an egoist conversation. In other words, by breathing in the truth, and exhaling the junk, we can easily have a conversation with anyone, who develops a loving and meaningful end to it.

Drama is the game the ego plays when it thinks we are not feeling its unhealthy energy. We find ourselves spinning with so many thoughts and conjuring up so many answers for ourselves that we envision everyone falling to their knees in recognition of our important mixed-up message. Our audience is usually those close to us, who have seen the same performance many times. We may forget that this performance gets bad reviews from our heart centers. We never feel good. We never get applause, and the theatre has no more than a few unfortunate people, who, somehow seem to handle bad dramas.

You should, we should, they should, are just other ways that the ego has us spinning with all the wrong answers. But, we seem to need to deliver the "I am right story" and "You need to agree with me" statements. When we finally exhaust ourselves and others, we realize that in order to keep the party going, we need another audience. If anyone tries to respond to us, or tries to fight back, we never hear them. All and all, in the end, we are exhausted and beaten down, not by the "right or wrong" of the situation, but by our unhealthy egos. Yes, our egos win again. We feel despair and embarrassment for saying way too much about nothing, or just plain embarrassment about the way we behaved. Our egos typically do not travel in healthy circles. In addition, they have the ability to let go, without overreacting.

So, the question is, in our own defense, have we ever given our egos permission to be such a renegade? We get caught in moments that have so much to say about something, and yet, many times nothing. Our breaths are stifled, and we are ready to defend, attack, and defend our own outlandish actions as reactions. So, the quick lesson is not to give our egos permission to control our conversations. In other words, stop the monster before it gets out of control. And, the only way to do that is to release our egos quickly, privately and with affirmative statements like: "You have no control." Breathe deeply, and you will be able to catch your truth, and release all that is not really relevant to you. *The chatter will subside.*

We let the tiger out of the cage, because we left it unlocked. It is difficult to stay on a continuous high watch. But, with practice and pain, and then, practice again, it becomes an automatic reflex. *Listening is always the key to a shutdown.*

Impeccable with our words is not part of our mantras, when our egos are hard at work. We would like to think we are doing our best, but, in reality, we are at our worsts. Many times, we fear being truthful, therefore we try stick to a few fragments of truth, but, truthfully, that truth is not an impeccable truth. Once again, our egos have been poised for attacks, and, as a result, they keep us under a spell of fear. In other words, we get caught in the dance of being seen and heard, all at the same time. This is totally insane. It causes us to experience uncomfortable residuals from the insane behavior. We have become a caustic combination of emotional outbursts, and a monkey running wild with insignificant pointless egoist chatter.

Outbursts and chatter are just other examples of emotional rags waiting to be released to the gift of spiritual riches. The good news is that they are always waiting in the wings. Our lives do not have to be complicated with half-truths, false situations, and bad advice, that is, ultimately, none of our business.

Our messy selves need a new way of living. It becomes evident, when we are finally alone, and have to review all of the nonsense that we have been distributing. That is when the lonely, sick feeling comes into play. We have work to do, but the work is not about others, no, it is about ourselves. We need to get on the bridge that will take us to spiritual riches. This is the time when we realize that we need to find ourselves. In other words, we need to find out who we really are, and what we really need. *We just need.* In fact, being needy can be the emotional rag that starts our journeys to our own spiritual riches. And, by just having quiet enlightened thoughts, we begin to heal. *This is the first personal miracle.* So, without even realizing it, we are on the hunt. This hunt finally gets us to the base of the bridge, which then delivers us to the other side, where we are gifted with everything that we need. We finally understand how to access all the things we need. These gifts await all of us, when we are ready. *We are already on the hunt for spiritual riches.*

Spiritual riches are a personal topic that replaces our old emotional rags. It is a re-birthing, but we are still ready to embark on new thought processes that will take us to a whole new life. *Just surviving no longer works.* We are here to learn a new way of thinking that fills our lives with hope, freedom, and authenticity. We are getting ready to understand what it will take to receive our rightful inheritance of spiritual riches.

The answer has always lived within us, and, now it is time to let the universe remind us of whom we really are. Do not be mistaken; it will take tools, time, and commitment. If we are really "ragged out," then, we are ready. If we are sort of "ragged out," we will be ready, once we receive the message that we want to change. *We want to be our change.*

There may have been a time, when a quick fix made us feels like we were on track with our quests for spiritual riches. Life can catch up with us, and our egos can catch us by surprise. We just forget. No worries. This formula never goes away. Only we go away, but can always return.

Exhausted with an old ways of thinking that continue to give us the same results, we find ourselves ready for a permanent vacation, in the arms of our true reasons for being on these soulful journeys.

A personal story:

I have so many stories about my ego. I was my ego. I lived, and died with this chattering menace that was my mentor. A mentor was always telling me not to tell anyone, who I was. People always told me to protect myself - from everybody. In other words, keep the story going, but make it about someone else. Put on a mask that looks authentic. It does not matter what is, but what does matter is what people think of it. With this kind of chatter, I always took things personally, which was not impeccable with my truth. Therefore, I was not able to do my best. In fact, I knew I was not doing my best. So, I stuffed it into my lower consciousness, and when this stuffed fact surfaced, I drank.

And, during my early years, as a child, I was taught behaviors that covered up everything. My family was all about hiding from the truth. In fact, they hid their smoking, mental illnesses, and abuse. Basically, they hid everything for from everyone, but they could not hide things from our neighbors, who heard it all, 24/7.

As result, I was well versed in hiding who I truly was. I was a very insecure. I also had very low self-esteem. I was a shadow of a person. And, as I grew older, and into my teens, I found out that I was different. I had a sexual attraction to boys. I hid that too. I never even admitted that to myself, until years later, after I had married a woman. When my truth finally came out, I blamed my marriage, and sexual orientation. But, truthfully, there was nothing wrong with my marriage. I was married to a wonderful, beautiful gal, who was very attentive to me, and who was very much in love with me. To this day, I am grateful for whom, she was, and to this day, I am deeply sorry for not understanding myself well enough to stop a marriage that should have never come about in the first place. But, it is what it is, and I have been willing to make amends for years, but it has just not been possible. A willingness to admit mistakes is all that is needed to make amends to others. So, if the other person is not willing to accept our apologies, well, our jobs are done.

It was not until years later that I even understood myself enough to realize that I was being controlled by my ego. It was not intentional, but my daily drinking habits kept my unhealthy ego at bay. But, unfortunately, there came a time when my daily drinking habits were not satisfying me anymore. *I had a choice.* I needed to first address my drug of choice, and then, the rest would follow, if I wanted to stay sober. *AA was a great help.* The 12-steps changed my life. The Big Book told me that I was not alone, and the members of AA supported my efforts to sober up. *I was raw.* Without the alcohol, my ego chattered away, without any way for me to shut it down. In order to stay sober, I had to follow the program to the letter. Surrender was first on my list, and reading the Big Book came next, along with securing a sponsor. A sponsor in AA is someone that a recovering alcoholic sees on a weekly basis. Sponsors have been sober for a long time. They are in service to those, who have a desire to stay sober. In addition, sponsors guide addicts through the recovery process by suggesting things (methods and techniques) that can help them remain sober. Ultimately, sponsors love you, until you can love yourself.

Next on the agenda of my new life, was to stay sober for 24-hours increments, go to meetings, and call your sponsor, if I wanted to drink. And, of course, I wanted to drink. *I was raw.* My ego would tell me, that it was OK to have just one drink. But, just one drink put me on the path to many drinks, and before long I was drunk again. So, now I had two big problems - staying sober and living sober. But, in time, with good direction, and attention to what I was supposed to be doing, I managed to put in some much-needed time towards improving my health. *What a good feeling that was!*

It was so good that, unfortunately, I drank again, in celebration. My ego kept telling me that I was spiritual because I had been able to stay sober for a long time. *What a mess I was in!* My ego, and its protective false ways, had a grip on me again. The next thing that happened was a full nervous breakdown. *That caught my attention.* It took many months to become sober again. *And, it was harder than ever before.* That was almost 16 years ago. Now, my ego can no longer talk me into anything.

When we become aware of the power our egos have over us, we are also shown the power we have to overcome their cunning ways. *I found the God of my understanding.* I became the truth of who I really was, so I started showing up to the life, I was meant to live. I learned so much about what worked. Now, I continue to learn what is needed and what works, in order to get my life back on track. If alcohol hadn't been the culprit, I would have had to overcome something else. That is how it works. We go through adversities to get us back on track. Once we get back on track, we end up having it all. *Amazing!*

Chapter Eight

The Treasure Hunt Begins!

WHEN ENOUGH IS ENOUGH. WHEN we want what we want, and we know that there is something out there, greater than anything we have ever thought, we could have. We are tapped on the shoulder, stopped in our tracks, and/or confronted with an enlightened. Spiritual riches begin with addressing our lives as they are NOW. When NOW becomes the most precious energy we could ever obtain, we are finally on to something big. This is what masses on this earth all covet, but it can only happen in the NOW. With our NOW comes the rest. Our good fortune and future arise during our NOW moments. During this time, we finally realize that we are here to live life fully, abundantly, openly, and with ease.

Does this mean we will be without problems or challenges? Are we to live, as if there is no tomorrow? No, in fact, there is a tomorrow, and there will be challenges and situations that will help us grow in the right direction. Without challenges, there will never be opportunities, and opportunities are what we ultimately seek. We want to discover the NOW. We want to become comfortably in-tune with our new thoughts, and a way of living that actually works. At this time, a shift in consciousness, that we can feel, occurs.

These new insights are different. They are not charged with the pity of emotional rags, like before, but they do light up a path that up until now, we had missed along the way. There will be recognizable lights, as we realize our willingness to just show up to what is right in front of us on a daily basis. The strain is gone. The help is in all the corners and cracks of the universe. *How did we miss this before? Where were we thinking or, better yet, not thinking? But,* all and all, we are right on time. We needed every moment up until now to get to our destinations. The goal is to be attuned to seeing the lights, and then, moving towards this natural universal ONENESS. In other words, when we are confused, we seek help. We learn to listen. We feel a tap on our shoulders. And, at this time, we sense a trust that we have never had before. We are in the beginning of a new ways of life. Yes, it takes some practice, but the teachers will appear, and the tools will arrive.

Our words will mean much more someday when we automatically accept this impeccable truth. Our actions will focus on the next right thing, sans the chatter of unhealthy egos. We are on our way, and the path is quite clear, as long as we stay clear. And, we will succeed with our full toolbox and a willingness to lead the way. Therefore, we automatically tap into intuitive connections, because they have always been with us. There will also be a new recognition of the God of our own understanding. Fear will not perforate our consciousness, rather, there will be an awe of the power, we now possess. This power allows us to create the life, we had been hoping for.

During this time, we realize that we have always needed a better understanding of this loving entity that we finally recognize. Finally, there is the God of our understanding, along with the recognition that we have guides and angels, along with loved ones, who are in the vapors of our lives. *We feel them.* We are intuitively connected to them, because we have learned to shut down and listen to our egos. It becomes obvious that we are growing into the mirror images of these co-creative energies. At that time, we realize the energy has always been there.

The energies we seek, and the energies we choose, are the energies we become. Our old fears of a vengeful God disappear. We are no longer judged, and punished by our higher power. Our God illuminates our levels of love. In other words, we no longer live with a God of pain, suffering, and wrath.

Truth-be-told, this way of thinking has been taught throughout the ages. We have been living in fear - of mans determined efforts to create judgment, and create power. Power and stress that many of us have had during our very hard, stressful lives. We have never been good enough. And, we never will be. This line of thinking only breeds others, who are not good enough, either. So, we find ourselves living in a world that is not good enough for any of us. This is not a successful way to be free of emotional rags. When we are caught in a trap of thinking that everyone else is not good enough, the trap changes and we end up in a snare of judging those, who are judging us. This becomes a horrific ride, spiraling downward, and leaving us in our own chaotic muddles.

This is a new day of enlightenment. There is so much light exposed in the universe, at this time, that the darkness is totally exposed. It may appear to be frightful, but, in reality, it must be exposed. The light is the goodness that has always won, and will continue to do so. It is our responsibilities to allow the loving consciousness to come through. The more goodness that seeps into the universe, the more armor is needed to overshadow and destroy what is not the truth of mankind. *We are Armageddon in the NOW. We are the warriors. We are the light.* And, what an honor to be the warriors of truth that show up in the NOW. We are the spiritual riches that come out of letting go of emotional rags. Our rags must go first, and the rest just IS. If we look at the history of mankind, and its connection to the universe, we will note that, under all circumstances, goodness always wins. We, then become the vapors of the universe do our part in the ONENESS. In other words, we become ONE with the enemy that is wounded and judging. But, with our light, we have join forces with the Spirit of God that lives within us. *We are doing our part.* It starts to become clear that we are living our lives the way the world meant us to. So, by keeping our own houses and thoughts clean, we become true spiritual warriors. We are free of rags and clothed in riches. And, by leaving judgment to the processes and outcomes of cause and effect, we are the ONES, with the very entities that judge us. Our ONENESS is the antidote to peace.

Personal Story:

I was lost, as a young man, so it took a long time to arrive at the "awakening state of a higher consciousness." But, looking back, I now see why it took so long. The timetable I was on was right on schedule. Fear was my biggest enemy. I was afraid of dying at Armageddon, God's war that is destined to eventually come and destroy the earth. At that time, all will go, except Jehovah's Witnesses. Then, there are those feelings – my attraction to boys. Oh, my God! I was for sure dammed NOW. And, then there was this thing that I knew was wrong. I told stories that put me out of the limelight so no one would find out my deep, dark secrets. This was the beginning of my many rags. My riches, at this point, may seem odd to most, but they worked for me. I got married, and then, I left the marriage, after finally telling another person that I was gay. I started going to gay clubs, and, during my first time out, as a gay man, I ended up staying in my car for an hour, trying to get the nerve to go in. When I finally did go in, someone grabbed my crotch in the coatroom. I proceeded to throw up, left, and did not return for many weeks. The key for me was to arrive with a few drinks, under my belt, which I did.

I was finally accepted somewhere. There were people, like me, where openly gay, and there were those, who were still hiding. Those in hiding were not open and honest about their lives. They snuck into back doors, just like me. And, once in that environment, they were free to be themselves. *Me too.* But, it wasn't until, drank beer, and more beer, and then, some more. Now, I was ready to interact. The alcohol comforted me. While intoxicated, I was likely to say and do anything.

I went home with many boys over a period of about a year. Then, I ran out of "unknown guys" to have sex. Truthfully, I didn't fully understand anything about having a serious, committed relationship with anybody. *Why?* Well, because I never had one with my own family. Therefore, I was not capable to of having a good marriage. I was just interacting with them for sex. It was the pre-AIDS era, and thankfully, I was spared from contracting the life-altering disease. I was free – totally free, and could not wait to get back to the bar every night to drink excessively, and hook-up with men. *I finally felt desirable and normal.* All my life, I felt out of sync – a real odd ball. But, not anymore. I was no longer separate from others. I was one of the guys. I was ONE with a community that accepted, who I was. Those were my first riches, and I needed them. There was no mistaking what I did, or how I did it. I had to come out, and I did in the best way possible for me.

There are a number of ways to change our thought processes, but it starts in that moment – the NOW. And, in order to keep the moment progressing in the right direction, we must pay careful attention to what we say, and what we are listen to. In other words, we need to learn how to show up to our treasure hunts, in order to claim our spiritual riches. Here is how it can begin to work.

Chapter Nine

Keep It Simple by Just Showing UP!

FIRST THINGS FIRST, ARE ALWAYS the best ways to start. Realize how funny you really are, and your humor will get you through anything. Everyone can learn to laugh at themselves (i.e. we discover our zipper is down or we have static cling in the crotch). *Oh well.*

Life is as serious, as we make it. Our journeys are important, when it comes to showing up. However, we are not so important that we do not need each other. *Oh, I can do it! No, thanks, but thanks anyway! Oh, I will figure it out. I really do not need anyone.* These are just tricks our egos use to make us believe that we are so important and self-sufficient, that we don't need anyone else. Truth-be-told, we may think so at first, but, in all honesty, we are never really alone, and we are unable to be alone, even if the insanity wants us to think we can. The universe does not work that way, never has, and never will. It takes everything - working with us, for us to clear the way.

It may take years for us to truly find ourselves, in the midst of change. It may take years for us to be ready to move on. We recognize in this NOW moment, that it is time to take a quantum leap. If we turn back, now, we will be forced to walk back into our old ways of doing things. We will revisit the same, old junk that has been in our lives for years. It is time for our messages to change. We thought we could change alone, we tried, and now, we need to take a quantum leap. Quantum leap is related to cause and effect. We are the cause, and create the effect. The scientific explanation is that we mathematically create action in our lives by stimulating the movement of atoms. In other words, we move with them, and thus, we are move out of what we are doing into something bigger and better for our overall goodness. This creates actions that are void of non-actions, and/or stagnations. It is also brought to light that it is time to let go of our emotional rags. It is time to trade them for our spiritual riches. This is another example of creating the cause to get the effect.

It takes a courage and faith to take a leap into something better for ourselves. It also helps us keep up our momentums. We have to be willing to keep on showing up by walking and staying in the present, with forward movements of commitment.

We all have guided help available, should we need it. And, then, there is our own willingness to the trust the process, under all circumstances. What we are witnessing in our lives is needed to bring us to our destinations. It is important not to get caught in imaginary illusive thoughts (i.e. what we think is happening). We don't know anything, until we see what is in front of us. We learn nothing, if we let our egos throw the past at us (predicting a gloomy, and/or fearful future). None of it is ever true. The truth always exists in the NOW. We are prepared to surface from lives of "what ifs" and "shoulds" to partake in lives of soulful ONENESS with our source and supply. Call this source and supply any name from any language, but know that your Higher Power lives within your higher self. Moreover, every soul that lives is connected to the greater good of everything else. Even in history, under horrific circumstances, we take note that goodness always wins. *ALWAYS.* We call up the good, and then, walk our walk.

We are teetering on the edge of our next cliffs, no parachute to let us glide to our new lives, yet there is always a safety net to catch us, should we jump, and not mean it. We are in the NOW of life. We jump off our cliff of dreams, dressed in a garment of hope and trust. At this juncture, we understand that we are just fine and happy. There is a new life that is ready to embrace us. That new life can be smaller or larger than others, who have jumped. But, this is not about others - This is about you. Our changed thought processes have set us up for changed lives. We all get to go the distance, and the distance is as far or near, as we are comfortable with. Many of us say that we have felt the nudge. Some may even say it was an invisible nudge, because we just jumped, without thinking. No matter how we get there, we are finally jumping. Thinking will never allow us to jump. It is when we stop thinking that we are able to scientifically respond to the movement. This movement is much like a reflex of the knee. *We just move!* And, because thinking is not a true motivator; we have little-to-no fear, which is good. Fear does not even come into play, as our reflexes take us to the next levels. We leap into the unknown. The deal has been done. And, now, the real fun begins. We are in the air, and life has become a daring adventure into the ONENESS principle. *The fear is gone.* What a spiritual gift that can only be explained by those, who have stopped being motivated by fear, and taken the long jump into the next levels of their lives.

We are surrounded with help from guides, loved ones that have gone on, and a Higher Power. We get the clarity that we have asked for. We are in need of those answers to keep going - walking of our new talk.

Some will tell us, "It won't be easy," but was it easy living in fear and lack? By, letting go of the fear, we find ourselves, surrendering with greater ease, and without egoist shame, because we did. And, maybe this is easier. We may actually find that our surrenders are the strengths that have changed our lives. In losing our controls, we are gifted with answers and intuitive thoughts that allow us to know how right we were about being wrong. Surrender and release provide us with the right to understand wrong, so that we can know what is right. The uneasy feelings in our stomachs have dissipated. We are no longer under the influences of unhealthy egos. Surrender has, once again, become the key to change.

There does come a moment, in this surrender, that we are elated and feeling good. And, then, without warning our egos try to rear their ugly heads to destroy our happiness. Our fears want to set in, but we no, have a warrior, who is fighting to keep them at bay. Our egos know why things do not work, in the big scheme of life. Our lives have changed; therefore, our egos have such small cracks to get through, that they would rather take acts upon themselves, so they can get back in. And, even if they do manipulate their way back into our lives, the stay is short. Our egos no longer have the power to withstand spirt-filled actions. They may try, but in the end, they will always lose, as long as we are stay connected to our source. And, if we walk what we have defined.

What if we surrender in front of others? Isn't that a sign of weakness our egos chant? *What do they think of me?* I must appear weak. Our egos would love for us to think that we are being watched closely by phantom bodies of people, or a mix and match of society, as a whole. It is interesting to observe how our egos become illusions of people, who no longer exist. Our egos consist of judgments, resentments, and self-doubts.

Spiritual warriors, who walk the walk, are quick to make decisions. *But, do they judge those, who are judging them?* Our newfound wisdoms allow us the freedom not to join the journeys of others. Their journeys are none of our business. We have much to do on our own paths. We do not have time to engage in other's lessons.

When we surrender, we may feel quite raw and venerable. It is our first times, so we are feeling our authentic selves. And, as we get used to this thing called "Being Real," it becomes easier to feel comfortable. We are not used to spiritual riches, yet! But, once we get it, the uncomfortable feeling will change to exhilaration.

But, even in our short-lived exhilarations, our egos jump in, informing us that we want proof of this new way of thinking, and the gifts our Higher Power has for us. We must always remember that our egos and addictive natures are very cunning and powerful, especially; if we internalize the messages they try to send us. Proof is not necessary, because as we show up to our lives, we are the proof.

We may show up in the right way, or we may show up in the wrong way, but the key is just to show up. We will be righted. We will be scooped up, and we will continue to make the choices, we have chosen. Truthfully, there is no right or wrong way to show up. We may choose a lesson or two, and then, find that the things that do not work in our lives is just other spiritual richness. We are showing up to our new lives! And, we are the ones doing it. Nobody else is changing us. We are changing us! Finally!

Being in the elated stance of what AA calls a "pink cloud," we do well for a time, and then after we think we are comfortable and all is well, without warning, we are back in the now what. We have been living our lives a certain way for a long time. We have walked paths that are much different, than the new ones, we are choosing. Of course, there will be some, that experience discomfort, but it will not last for long, especially, if we recognize it and return to the basics. Showing up to the next right thing is a basic need. In other words, even when everything seems strange, once we admit to our truths, we will become authentic and transparent. Disturbing feelings will disappear.

And, even if our new spiritual garments feel too tight, and our old garments feel way too baggy, we still get the "yin and yang" of new thought processes. We may feel messy and relieved – all at the same time. Again, we are witnessing spiritual richness. It is rather young and ne, but it is definitely becoming on us. We have joined or rejoined the dance of this lifetime, and we are taking the leads. The floor is huge, and we know how to keep our dance cards full. *All is well.*

All IS.

To help us, as we grow, we need to know that the beginning of our surrenders is the beginning of knowing that we can ask for help. *Why is it that so many cannot ask for help, but have the answers for so many others?* We all need help at one time or another. Our spiritual gifts are able to arrive more quickly. Help is on the way, and is the way. Giving and receiving go hand-in-hand.

If we really need help, and we settle down in the silence, we can hear the small, still voice that lives within us. We stop ignoring the messages. We no longer have the fear to follow through on what is coming through our heart chakras.

Once again, and as many times as needed, we pull out the hat that says we are willing to accept new ways of thinking. Our emotional rags can be appreciated for what they were, and then, let go. We have chosen new ways of thinking, and the results are always manifesting, sometimes quickly and sometimes slowly, but always manifesting.

Seven Steps to Obtaining Our Spiritual Gifts:

1. SURRENDER
2. Start Showing Up!
3. Acceptance
4. Willingness
5. Trust
6. Faith
7. Gratitude

This may sound easy - I can do that. - I am that. But, it is important to remember that if we were all that, we would not need numerous lessons to help us find our ways. They are ways that are no longer chaotic, but peaceful. Ways that work, when we work at it. Lives that starting to become what they are meant to be. Yes, it can be easy, but only if we are truly ready to embark on new thought processes. The deaths of our old ways of thinking are imminent.

Without tying ourselves to our pasts, and refusing to look towards the future, we lose opportunities to have it all. We are not meant to have everything, but we are meant to have it all. That means having all that we need and all that we want. And, all that needs to take place for us to have the necessary energies circling us, so we are in line waiting to proceed with spiritual sacred contracts. We can have it all! We just have to KNOW it, BELIEVE IT, and stay intimately attuned with our Higher Power, and the small still voices that live, within each of us. The trust we have in this process is done by the faith. Forces that truly have our backs are guiding us. It takes what it takes to go where we are going, so we just need to stay out of its way.

Our egos like to ambush us. Our jobs are to know that our egos are out of a job, once we fire those unforgiving menaces. We can claim our strengths, and become stronger, because of our ONENESS connections. We constantly refer to the ONENESS, and this gives us the walk that goes with our talk, on a 24-hour basis. We are learning new ways of thinking. In fact, we are really starting to walk our talk!

Surrender:

So we had it rather tough growing up. We felt abandoned. We felt that we were not loved. Our brother always got the Fruit Loops and we had to be raisin counters and were always hungry…oh well. When we get caught up on what happened in our youth, our teen years, and our early 20s, we are nowhere even near our present moment. We are in our past - a past that is gone and cannot be changed. And we may still have some deep seated resentments now and if they are not resolved, we might have them at age 80.

At 80 we may forget because we may be forgetting everything anyway. But the lessons are never over until they are over. We may take lifetimes to change the way we think, or we may take this lifetime. This is the lifetime in which we are facing some important changes regarding how we live and how we think. Are we ready? We most likely thought we were before we arrived. But are we ready now to embark on changes that will give us new hope, new freedom, and a Higher Conscious Self so that we can evolve to our next level of mindfulness in practice? Eternal we are. It would be comforting to think that we could accomplish at least some of our goals as we walk through another lifetime of immense information and access to our Spiritual Gifts that have been waiting for us. It is so true that we will live to yet another lifetime of rebirth to address all that we put aside in this lifetime. How fortunate we are that we are not discarded but embraced whenever we are ready to travel to our next level of consciousness.

Our past is our past. It is gone. It can only be a learning tool for the present moment, which naturally on its own has the option to build a successful, productive, and abundant future. The Now is our future in progress. Our good future depends on our NOW. This life can be so much easier by just showing up in our moment and doing whatever the next right thing is. The questions always posed are "What is in front of me?" "What is my next right step of action?" And then…no dilly dallying. Those who have aspirations to Higher Thought know to just do it! Just Show UP! No more waiting. No more pushing things aside. It becomes much easier to just address our NOW moments. Our future reaps the benefits and the rewards.

When we have not surrendered to anything, we find ourselves whining, stamping our feet, complaining, feeling depressed, angry and despondent. It's okay to change our diapers and move on to the next level of potty training. Staying in a dependency of infantile baby tantrums is not growing spiritually. We are here to grow to a Higher Level, to recognize we are here to be ONE with a Power much greater than we are. There is a recognition that takes place where we feel the ONENESS because we are accessing a pure and loving communication with our Higher Power. We have finally learned to listen.

Yes, some of our past is frustrating, irritating, and maddening. But there comes a time when those hurts need to be addressed, defined, and gone…they have to go. If we are to move on to our next great thing, our next great experience and our next right incarnation, there comes a time when we are asked throughout God Center to let it go. Our heart knows. We know. Spirit knows. If we do, the hurts and discomfort we experienced will not be able to repeat themselves - unless we keep letting the voice in our head take over once again. That egotistic voice loves the drama and keeps the ego well fed and keeps the soul in need out of rhythm with the only thing that can change a life successfully: the God of our understanding, a voice of truth that comes through from our angels, guides and loved ones. We are deaf until we have mastered the quieting of our ego.

The truth becomes apparent by the way we feel. When we need to move on, adversity and change is but an illusion of good things to come. But we have to let go. There is no other way of the Spiritual Warrior to accomplish the battle of the ego, which produces addiction, dysfunction, fear, anger, and loss of the life the Soul is here to live. We can let go. We can. Opportunity will surface like a warrior on a white horse of a victorious battle. The ego and the heart, until tamed, make a tenacious battleground. However, with attention to the heart, addressing opportunity in the NOW, we leave adversity behind. It's automatic. It will happen without trying and without struggle. It's the way of the Spiritual Warrior. It's the way to the treasure that has long awaited us. We are gifted with many Spiritual Riches once we win our battle of egotistic self run riot.

A Spiritual Warrior knows how and when to review a haunting past as a prerequisite to letting it go permanently. The warrior in us feels when it is time. With the discipline to be quiet, we can access the voice of stillness that comes through with authority and loving direction. This is not a fearful voice. It is always found to be in our best interest to heed the voice of stillness. It is the Divine Light illuminating our path.

We are allowed to come to believe with certainty that it is what it is, and the NOW moment we are accessing is perfect and whole. Being human, having a spiritual experience may find us still asking ourselves why. Knowing that our answers live within, taking ownership of quieting down once again for the guidance of our Higher Power is one of the Riches we can now call upon. We will access the NOW and let the days of old thinking and worn out habits dissipate and die. With this attitude and clear thinking, it is nearly impossible to be a victim. But the self does display itself as a more peaceful Spiritual Warrior on track and a warrior of action.

The speed with which we surrender those years to a time of growth and opportunity will help us to keep making all needed changes. Change is always certain. Do we have to go it alone? No, and in all honesty, those who have tried have rarely found success. But those who tune in and access the help that is available to all soar with lives of abundance and prosperity. No one is to be left out. We all may have the gifts of Spiritual Riches. So it is a decision; everyone gets a chance. Deciding to go it alone or ignore what is ours to have is a great way to by-pass an opportunity of sanity. Nirvana escapes those who choose not to have it…yet.

By learning how to check in daily and listen to our still small voice that lives within, we become addicted to the clear messages that give us our NOW answers. These are messages in truth that ensure our well-being. If we have never really accessed the still small voice, we will still be searching for the way to peace. Everyone wants their own peace of mind.

But in the quest for Nirvana, we often get we captured by the egotistic monkey mind chatter that has us in a whirlwind where we are unable to make clear decisions. The chatter has too many voices for us to determine what voice to listen to and what our next right thing to do is. We are definitely not reaping the rewards of our quest for Spiritual Riches. Instead we are still in a mentality of Emotional Rags. That can change.

If we never are willing to let go, ask for help, and surrender, we prolong the wait for good health and our continued on-going mind body and spirit healing. However, our Higher Power, our buddy, our best friend and the Highest Source we can go to will wait for us with amazing fortitude. Some may say God is a patient God...but God does not have to be patient because God in the biggest sense has never been impatient. Our Source and Supply is there when we are there.

Once again we will find a Universe that loves us and we will get to have as many false starts as it takes to get where we need to be able to access a life of Spiritual Riches. Emotional Rags are just part of the journey. They are needed so that we know more about non judgment of others as well as how to access our own self-love. When we are offered a choice and it elevates pain, we are forced to stay the same. In that moment of truth, we are offered a choice to elevate pain. We are here to have and live better, and have the life we are meant to have. It will always be up to us, and it will come with a personal relationship with the God of our understanding. There is no one in the Universe that can ever fix us. They may carry our burden with themselves. They may control us with the notion that we are being saved from ourselves. But in the end, the only way to save ourselves lives within us. The only way to save others is to tell them about the voice that lives within them too.

It's not as risky to surrender as we might surmise. It may feel that way... as fear seems to always rear its ugly head when we come to a point of knowing that we need to let go and surrender our question to something bigger, higher, and more capable to help us. And then we are back to that still small voice that is the God of our understanding coming through loud and clear or quiet and penetrating. By not taking what we think is a risk, we will never know, nor will we have our answer. We can keep trying, or we can retreat to our same old way of living and our same old results. It may take our first try or our second try or our 50th try. It is not how many times that we need to show up to make our surrender stick, it is that we stay focused and willing right to the end. The gifts await us in our surrender. The message is don't give up. Show up and let your life show up to you. You are in charge of your own surrender.

In the moment of surrender, the ego is caught off guard, stunned and dumfounded, totally immobile and disconnected and unable to chatter. Our surrender saved a precious moment. We feel the ease and the peace and NOW know that fear had no strong-hold.

Chapter Ten

Acceptance Is the Key to Your Kingdom!

IT IS YOUR KINGDOM. IT is a Kingdom that we make by the way we think. Acceptance to what is, is absolutely the key to making sure our kingdom is not taken over by a band of egotistic run-a-way Shoulds and What Ifs. They are always lurking but are powerless voices of the ego when acceptance to what is takes center stage. The Shoulds are tied to the ego, totally unable to function if they are not consulted. They do not have the keys unless you hand them off; just know the ego wants those keys. The What Ifs keep hanging out with The Shoulds, but unless you hand off the keys to unlock the ego, they are totally disabled. The bridge is up and the walls are secure. The Shoulds and the What Ifs are no longer empowered by our letting them come through in our conversations.

In the course of a day in the life…we may find ourselves living as a daytime soap… The World Turns into the Edge of Night. Drama is always a key player in recharging the ego. And the ego is ready at a moment's notice to jump ship and get back in the game of taking control and sending out the messages of doubt and fear. But with acceptance of what is, we find ourselves not engaging in reacting to the soap operas of others or the ones that pop up quickly in our life. In our on-going course of learning our lessons, we are will realize that we are doing minimal reacting to people, places, and things. We are accepting, letting go, and living in the moment of "what is."

Acceptance means we accept the IS without leaving ourselves open to having our good energy stolen. The IS is our NOW. If we are tuned into the NOW, chances of catching us off guard with other people's drama is quite impossible.

By accepting life in the NOW and just noting that we are not the problem, we quickly are relieved of Energy Vampires. They are not able to drag us in because by being aware we will not allow them in. Quickly we surmise that what others are doing or saying becomes none of our business…thank God! There is no need to even judge those who want us to fall into the trap of their energy sucking drama. So unless we walk into the trap that is ready to snap away our peace, we cannot be snared. It can only be sprung if we are not aware. But is not being aware once again the acceptance of what is right NOW?

Accepting life on life's terms with all its twists and turns can be challenging, but once we have developed the tools of acceptance, we find it easier to just let much of life be. It really is what it is, and the IS of life will change. It has to. And if we let it be…it will be as it is intended to be without our ego's control or supervision.

Patience and just being present to our moments are all part of accepting. Becoming healthy, we will find that when life is not a roller-coaster, it can feel rather strange. We may even feel as if we were missing something. It could be that we have not lived without the extremes of ups and downs. It can almost seem frightening until we have grown accustomed to ourselves without the high drama. It may take some time, but time is what and why we are here. We are blessed with an opportunity to learn. Our lessons are wonderful, hard and still wonderful. Without the lessons we could not be a part of this thing called time. Now we have a choice in our NOW, to exit our run-a-way rollercoaster and step on to a safe platform that is anchored to the next right thing to do, proving that there are not bad lessons just great opportunities.

Sometimes it takes conscious effort to slow down. And then if we do not cooperate with our intuition that nudges us to slow down, we are forcibly slowed down by a loving Universe. This slowing down period is nothing more than reminding ourselves that we are in need of letting go. Our thinking has been on an egotistic rampage and we are unable to hear what is best in the next moment.

All we think we may be missing is just a downhill spiral or the upward climb saving us before we plunge to an unavoidable bottom that we seem destined and determined to hit. We can still go there, but we will get indicators several times before we have to embark on a lesson that could have been avoided.

So, there will be definitely times that we can hear the message of slowing down, and then there are other times that there is no message possible that can break through our self-will run riot mode. We are now at the bottom and for good reason need to start that upward climb to learn exactly what no longer works in our life. It is a gift to know. We will find that out later after we have stopped stomping, crying, and feeling sorry for ourselves. There comes a day when we have a story of success to share that started out looking like a disaster.

It may or may not feel odd that we got stopped right in the middle of an obsessive controlling thought that we are not willing to let go. But like with all Emotional Rags, the Universe has the last say and if we surrender will give us favor and protection. We later learn it was the only way we could have even hoped to be stopped. We are given the benefit of choice, even in bottoming out. Any change of thinking whether it be surrender or acknowledgement of where we are is the start of healing. The Spiritual Riches await us.

Accepting this down time has its benefits. It becomes a time to rejuvenate, spend more personal time in meditation, and give further attention to the practice of being still. By learning to listen, we find the Now in our life if not by choice but through the rags of emotion or by accident. Something clicks and the cloud lifts, and we are totally elated. We have the bounce back in our step. The gloom lifts. The quandry about what to do is totally gone. We have our answers. Yes there will be a change in thinking to be made, but we will feel ready. There is plenty of proof that this is true, but the only way to understand this experience is through a lesson that puts us into the front of the line for Spiritual Richness is to show up, trust, and have faith in ourselves that we can stick to our new thought with anticipation of a new life that is now coming to fruition. We ask our new questions knowing that we already have the answer. We listen, and the proof is manifested.

Personally, I will share with you that for years I have always had a difficult time when life slows down. I feel like I am missing something. And I found out I was right on. I was missing the time that I needed to just be. I was missing my chaotic running and doing just to look and feel busy in a worthy way. I was a demented robin always trying to get one more worm. I was so full of worms that I could not sing my way into spring. I found through this valuable lesson that I did not need all those worms - just one at a time. I was much better prepared to show up for my next right thing instead of 50 wrong things first. However, even many times in my waiting I was still needed to check in as I wanted to run and do nothing of great importance. I was busy with busy. How many times can you wash a car, sweep a floor, or cut your grass? I had an odd combination of guilt and success. If I did not look busy, I was not productive. If I was productive I needed to be busier. Thank God there is a softer, easier, saner way. I am exhausted just writing about my old crazy ways. Today I listen. Today I do not apologize for being tired or wanting to read a book, take a walk, or just sit and be. I am allowed to have all of life…not just the "watch me work…aren't I something else??"

It was quite a change from being a doer so you or they or whoever would think I was worth something. I had to find my own worth and then if you found it too…great we had something in common. The vacations I take today are by the minute, by the hour, by the week or by the month. I stop when I need to stop. So when life gives me some free time, it is because I am willing to take it. There is absolutely no cure when we are unwilling to slow down or stop. But by my own admission to staying obsessively busy like a nonstop locomotive, the Universe always stepped in and slowed me down to a crawl. When my back went out sometimes I could not even crawl. Today, I would rather spend my free time on the beach or in a museum as opposed to trying to crawl to the bathroom. Slowing down was just being present to the moment. I am grateful for that lesson.

My lessons with impeccable truth have continually reminded me to let my reading audience know that I have had my slips too in moving fast and furious. But today with my antennas up and my intuitive connected to my God Source, I usually catch myself. If not, do I need to tell you where I cannot crawl to? I never want the bathroom to ever again feel like a destination property out of the country. Instead, I value the still small voice that gives me my messages. I want to know what my next move is or my next right thing to do should be. So, now I do it. I have become willing to take the High Watch of my own life and strive not to fall into old worn out behaviors. It is a beautiful to gift of Spiritual Richness to leisurely walk in the woods or on beach, to pick up a fun book on adventure or history or something we want to read for pleasure. In my own spiritual work that I am doing, it is good to remember, everything is spiritual, even that English mystery or science fiction tale of other worlds. We are alive and with Spirit every minute. That good book that is a mystery is as spiritual as our last daily word. We start noticing the messages in all things. And by the way, taking a nap or going to a movie can bring a Spiritual Message we never expected.

We are all a spiritual experience on various levels in the journey. Be it the agnostic, the atheist, or a monk...we all get messages and they change our lives and our directions. The Universe is of ONE defined being and we are all connected. No matter what we are or what we are doing, we are getting spiritual messages. What we choose to do with these acts of kindness or valued lessons is totally up to us. Spirit IS...WE ARE planetary atoms and molecules and energy in action. We choose our high or low vibrations.

Just because we take a daily reprieve from our daily routine does not mean that we have become lazy or lackadaisical. A message of a slower pace gives us insights so that when we are in high gear, there is nothing to think about. We are a walking channel of energy, and we can accomplish anything that has been put in front of us. Just one more Spiritual Richness.

So here is a concluding thought on acceptance as an important Spiritual Gift to obtain: just know that when life throws us a few curves, and it will, let us try to accept what IS that is in front of us and remember to keep showing up! But most importantly, let's try to keep our focus on listening and showing up to the next right thing. With this easy principle, our lives will stay on track on connected to the God of our understanding. We will find that we are living in the Oneness of Spirit and there is nothing we cannot do or have. This is an incredible Spiritual Gift.

Chapter Eleven

Willingness
(Willing to be willing)

THIS THING CALLED WILLINGNESS IS about walking our talk. By showing up we become willing to walk our talk. It is a commitment that changes our life one day at a time. Without willingness, our talk and our walk are just not in sync. In the practice of cause and effect, there is no way we can cause a new situation to take place in our life if we are not willing to intentionally commit.

There are many times we may say we are willing but when the rubber hits the road…our brakes are locked and the only thing we are willing to do is to be unwilling. We are scared! We may not know it, but fear has found a crack in our energy field. We are so stuck and yet so ready for a positive change. We talk about it. We have quick starts. We over dramatize why we can't do what we said we would do. Because we just are not willing.

Willingness comes with Action to Engage. It is quite simple, but it has to be embraced fearlessly. Trust and faith work then committing to leaving out hope can help. Hope is future thinking. If we hope we will, we won't. Although there is a hope that could work… if we have hope to succeed, we will then move to trusting the process, but our hope has to be acknowledge in our NOW.

By the acknowledgement of hope in the NOW we are already doing so. We have the faith in ourselves every time we commit in the

NOW. We do not have to be desperate to change our world; we just need to change it. We can be desperate, but that is an unnecessary choice that we sometimes make to motivate ourselves to go after a goal that could have been reached in a much shorter time.

Faith is not separate from our faith that we develop with our Higher Selves the Higher Power of our understanding that lives within us. We do realize that when we are willing, we are ONE in Action. Showing up becomes much easier! However, it does require a Higher Conscious effort to keep the momentum of showing up until it becomes automatic for us to show up to our next right thing. But that's what willingness is all about. As we show up to our dream, goal, or thought, it will willingly show up to us.

This is the way that always works, Show UP. It's simply Just Showing UP! As we are living our life on life's terms, a new way of thinking is nudging us. We can accept the inevitability of change or live fearfully losing freedom feel how alive we really are. There will be times when change is blatant and there are times when the need to change takes on a more subtle nature. But when it is time to Show Up to our next right thing, we will be filled with all the necessary willingness if we want the life we have been dreaming about. Our job is to recognize it and start listening. We will be led. This is how the Universe works when we have learned to listen and to be ready.

For many of us there have been many times when we were unhappy with our life's circumstances even when we had learned from past experience how cause and effect works. The Emotional Rags were evident, and we seemed to be repeating behaviors. We wanted change. Again. We may even have been asking everyone, again, what we knew intuitively to do. And again we were reminded that the person who always knows what is best for ourselves is ourselves. We always have the answers and as has been stated millions of times, by Buddha, "When the student is ready, the teacher will appear." At this juncture we are already teachable by just showing up. We ask why, and yet we always know deep within us our own answers. We know we want a better way to think and live, and we know it is available.

Being willing to the "What IS" in front of us, is a great valiant start. However, there is more involved as we soon realize we need to be an open vessel so we can absorb the truth coming through on a soul level through our heart.

Once we acknowledge and are willing to experience the "IS" in our lives we have many possibilities. We get to decide what our day will look like. But more importantly we get to decide how our day is to feel. If we are experiencing untreated depression we will not know what or how to feel thus keeping our lives at bay. So decisions need to be made, be it a doctor's appointment, a meditation, a prayer. But we are in need of action. Our life cannot unfold until we have recognized and treated depression whether it is clinical or brought on by life's circumstances. There are some who have a DNA issue with depression and are prone to periods of deep downward mood swings. However, in a world of ONENESS and availability to pure energy brought to us by the talents of the doctors who treat depression, we are encouraged to seek out this God Given Care brought to us in the medical field. Once we are treated, we also have the spiritual tools as well as the benefits of science to help us rise above and beyond thoughts that are not part of our soulful journey. Our Emotional Rags of depression are the road to Spiritual Riches if we know what is necessary to treat a disease that can take our life away.

A personal story:

I was one of those people that had undiagnosed depression. From a very young age, I was in a state of sadness. I always felt down and the low energy readings that I gave off were very detectable especially by other young boys and girls that were healthy. I was subjected to bullying. My depression was untreated until after I turned 45 when by accident I was being treated for what I thought was a heart attack when in reality it was anxiety and depression. I had suffered for years with low self-esteem and high anxiety. I found my fix to correct these feelings in alcohol. It was the only way that I could be relieved of this intense and menacing disorder. Thank God I did not add drugs to the mix. It is a hard situation to try and explain unless one has been through the cycles of high anxiety and depression.

At times I found that I could not think clearly, make rational decisions or move to the next right thing. I was full of fear. Alcohol took the fear from me and added impulsive decisions that many times were wrong. I was always second-guessing myself. My work was always shrouded with a hyper blood-sucking energy that made me feel defensive and never good enough. The rest of any energy that was left I used to maintain a voice and a presence behind my illusive curtain. My presenting self was programed to hide what was going on with me on a daily basis. People would not understand. They would judge me. They would find out that I was not good enough. The "theys" were frightening demons, and if they ever found out that I was depressed and living an undercover life with alcohol would abandon me. Even with alcohol, I had been abandoned many times as a child and again as an adult. I had to keep my secret life under wraps.

Today I am free of the depression and anxiety. But it took being willing to be treated for it. It took willingness to stop the drinking and face my demons. And as far as the people I thought would not understood, surprisingly they did. And the ones that did not I found that I did...oh well. Many times it came common knowledge later on that they were fighting their own demons. How would I have known? I was so busy hiding mind. My life started getting better as I was sober and began the process of addressing one by one the many haunts of the past. I have to acknowledge how wonderful the Twelve Step Program was for me. I already was spiritual in nature, but the simplicity of doing the steps in order gave me what I needed as I embarked on a life without alcohol. Of course it was more than alcohol I was overcoming. I had stuffed years away in the back of my mind. The years were surfacing and I had the tools to allow me to address why I drank like I did.

When I found out that I had levels of anxiety and depression that were manifesting as heart disease, I remember telling the doctor, "I am fine. My life is good." Why am I having these feelings out of the blue? It was a family disease and my DNA was set up to take on the disease of alcoholism. It came through not only on my father's side of the family, but my mother's as well. My Dad had been sick for years with mental illness. It was mental illness spurred on with drugs and alcohol. I began to understand why he did what he did and why he turned out to be what he was. He was hiding too. But like him, I had to decide to take the next right step. He was not willing and lived a life of horrific depression, pain, and mental illness until he took his own life at the age of 63. He took his own life by jumping out of a 13 story assisted living building. My compassion is ever so present as to what he had to endure all those years of being so undiagnosed and trying so hard to live in a world that was foreign to him. I lived there too. But at this time in medical history, he did not get the kind of care that could help. He was drugged and drugged again just to keep him quiet when he finally ended up in a mental hospital. No one knew at that time what to do for these people. And without alcohol in the hospital he was first admitted to, he was raw with untreated emotional scars. It had to be very scary for him. I was of little help as I was young and had been so abused by him that I was at a loss as to what to do. I followed directions and got him into a mental hospital as he had tried to commit suicide more than once. Today he would have had a better chance if he was willing to address all the horrors that kept him so sick for so long. So does this thing called willingness have to do with my story?

There are daily tools that can put us on the cutting edge of finding our willingness and then keeping it. By learning the art of meditation and affirmative prayer we find that our old way of fearful thinking goes away. When we are willing to listen in our NOW moment, we find how willing we are to fearlessly move forward and then "stay in" place waiting for continued God Direction to take us to our next right step.

By doing what is in front of us, no matter how big or how small, we will find answers coming through our Heart Center. The answers have always been there. We just needed to be on time with willingness. It became time to begin to recognize what we thought was our *problem* is really our *question*. The answer appears once the question is asked. We could say..."Oh my God that is a miracle!" Yes, at first it appears to be because we have never used this newly found ancient formula to solve our questions. And even if we knew about this formula, it takes us time just to continue to become aware. And sometimes we even have to go through a lesson of bottoming out. But once again being in an Emotional Rag will give us our Spiritual Riches just by being willing. Just by being willing. That's all it takes to get the Universe in motion to answer and guide us into our next right thing. Once you have put this into practice, what you once thought of as a miracle becomes commonplace. Without discounting a miracle, it may be rightfully said that our miracles have been going on since the beginning of time and now we are recognizing that our whole life has been and is a miracle. We are living and breathing in the vapors of Universal Understanding. We are ONE. What a gift to behold.

So what happens when the ego takes its turn again right after you go through the last surrender on something that you needed? It does take some conscious effort to calm down the overbearing monkey mind of the ego. But taming that beast is the first step to listening. The ego only has the control we give it. Once you know this there will be an inward calming effect that will take the place of the chattering ego. It is so calming that we can finally hear that still small voice leading the way to our once mind-rattling ego that loves to keep us in doubt and fear. The answer has always been there and is fighting to get out. And we get to know! With no separation from our God, the fight for truth is available. We will have to listen to get the riches promised in our spiritual ongoing existence.

If an Emotional Rag needs to be healed…the fastest approach is to just heal it with willingness. For any moment of panic and doubt, we finally ask that question that we have had no answers to. The simplest way to know that we have our answer is to listen, let go, let God, and let the answer come on time exactly when it will be the most advantageous for all concerned. This is not a "Me" principle. Being part of the whole helps us to recognize that our answers are always on time when the time is right. Our job is always to let go and let it happen under God Power and Our Power. With affirmative action, there is no separation from our Source and Supply. Together we will have all that we need. A Doubting Thomas just needs to take the jump and try the only exercise that has the best results when answers come to questions asked.

If by some fearful chance we still cannot seem to listen, no spiritually driven answers can appear. Our head will jump around with the ego and the confusion and indecisive beginnings. There is never any room for soulful answers. They are squeezed out by an over active, chatty Kathy of an ego.

In the continued effort to not let the ego get the upper hand, we turn to the one sure thing we have always had and will always have our Higher Power. We will find once again that the answers to our questions are coming to us in the increments needed to get us to the final solution with all the other souls that are to be involved in our Spiritual Riches. The answers can come from almost anywhere. It may be a quiet thought or it may come through in a song on the radio. It could be on a billboard while driving home from work. Or maybe a long lost friend has contacted us for a conversation that contains the exact message we need to hear. And do not discount an article that we happen to pick up in a waiting room at a doctor's office where an out of the blue message jumps out to our rescue. Nothing is by accident when we are present to our moments. When the ego is not in play, when we are in our present NOW moment, the answer comes and is on time.

Because we live in a world of ONENESS, our answers will continue to come right on time. This also reinforces that we are all in this thing called life together. As the planets, the moon and the sun everything when left alone is moving in perfect synchronicity. Timing is always right for the answers to our questions. When we realize what that the simply is of our lives just IS, we get the answers with soulful intuitive direction. It is humbling in our moment of discovery to attest to a force that has such power and lives within us.

A peaceful presence comes over our beings because we are in a ONENESS Arena where we know that we know that we know. What is this knowing? We have automatically let the question go direct. We stop questioning and know that the answer will come. Automatically we return to our NOW addressing only what is in front of us. The time lapse of letting the thinking game take us over becomes almost non-existent and if it does show up we are quick to let go and let God. Our assurance that the answers will come is our NOW welcome reality. No longer is there a need to get stuck in future or past thinking, let alone the illusion of what we think is happening in our NOW. Gratitude sets in as the still small voice of non-reaction takes over and guides us to solutions that we used to find ourselves lamenting over. It is a time of realization of how fortunate we are; free from the obsession of an egotistic mind. Life has changed and is so much better and easier.

The ego has lost its power. The agitation, high and lows, or fears of the ifs and the shoulds are no longer with us in the form of pre-conceived doubt. The bag of tricks that the ego has used for years is empty and high drama is a surfing channel that has gone off our flat screen. Spiritual Riches has given us programing that is more individually suited to our life and the life we are here to gift.

So the question in the NOW that often comes up is: Are we willing, really willing to change the way we accept acceptance. Yes or No…are we willing? We know there is no reason not to be willing, but will we move forward and except a new way of thinking? This is where faith comes in. Not in the religious dogma of doctrine but the faith we have living in our souls that is ready to be set free. To have this faith and access it, we need to know that it exists and then simply become the faith that we are. Looking for faith, asking for faith only tells the Universe that it is non-existent to us. A perfect God gave us all that we need to believe and have the faith of knowing that we know. It lives within us and we get to have it at any time we choose. Yes, asking may still be required when needing direction, but faith is one of our biggest tools of discovery. We can move to that mantra in the face of any challenge quickly once we realize that it is there and always has been. In a ONENESS principle we have the tool of faith. God is Faith. We are Faith. Just as we are the I AM of this life. Our I AM is the statement of truth that is used to stand together in ONENESS yet be the perfect self-expression of the Universe. "So may your insightful nudge come to you and may you know that because you are perfect and whole, faith is your likeness to the God of your understanding." With faith, we are always winning at being willing. Now we can win at this thing called willingness.

Chapter Twelve

Unshakeable Trust Beyond Trust

Do you or did you not trust your parents? Do you or did you not trust your partner/spouse? Do you trust your employer and the people you work with? Or not? Did you or do you trust yourself? We can never trust anyone until we finally trust ourselves. If we want the ability to trust we must find out if we are authentically trustworthy. Are we transparent about who and what we are? Or are we living a life where we do not trust anyone because if we do the trustworthy lifestyle is mirrored back to us? And what does it take in our own lives to start letting others know us? With questions such as these we are in a real wake-up call. And as all lessons…this is good.

It has been said that the best place to start is at home with who we really are. We are the only ones that can take on this very important self-inventory. Nobody knows us better and nobody can change the way we trust or do not trust except for ourselves.

Some easy questions to ask are, "Am I transparent enough to be truthful? Do I assume that everyone is out to get me? Am I afraid to let people know who and what I really am? Have I accepted myself in all areas of my life? That would include my strengths and weaknesses. Am I done hiding?"

With these few questions, we can assess our lives quickly. There may be some areas that we can answer affirmatively and others that we hang our heads over or ignore. But until we find ourselves, we will never be able to trust anyone fully. We will always doubt that others do not have our best interest at heart. We are not willing to be open, honest and trusted, so why would we consider that anyone else would? This is a time to have our own best interest at heart.

Once we have finally been willing to take a good look at who we really are, or are not, we are ready to embark on a journey of transparency and authenticity.

By acceptance of all our good and all that we would like to change, we get closer to a ONENESS Principle that we will not be willing to lose. By accepting the next right thing with both the good and bad that we are...we are closer than ever to experiencing a ONENESS with Divine. At this point we may come to an understanding and have an opportunity of willingness to open up and start trusting others. When you know yourself so well, trusting others is no big deal because you are transparent and whole. Whatever they may say about you is true because you told them what your truth was. This becomes an exciting time of enlightenment. Who can hurt you now? No one.

The most important part of trust is not only admitting all that we are, but then just showing up to our lives every day as a open truthful authentic being. Because we are present with integrity we can trust others and be trusted. We attract safe trusting people to share our open ended story.

And if the time should arise that we need help with finding trust in another, it will never be a problem, but it will be a question that we automatically take to the still small voice that lives within us. The truth will show up because we have become truth. We are living truth, and we have learned to trust our intuitive to guide us. We can accept that we have something bigger and better helping us. Our angels, loved ones, the great masters and guides are among us to channel information to help us in this lifetime. Never alone and always connected, we remain on high alert and allow our answers, sacred contracts and points of service to show up committed to listening.

GRATITUDE BEGETS GRADITUDE

If life is not working…your way, how wonderful. What a great opportunity to be grateful. Life seems to be going along great and much is happening to make it better. What a great time to be grateful.

Gratitude is knowing that you know everything that is happening for you and to you is something to be grateful for. If there is strife, stress, and loss in your life, how in the world would you think that you could be grateful? Maybe you cannot at the time, but it comes later. We need changes, and upheavals in our life to sometimes make us change for our own good. Stress is an indicator that we need to change our life and change our thinking. For this we can be grateful. Strife is annoying and hard to live through and as we change our thinking, we can find a way out. And this will be a better way for us in the long run. For this we can be grateful.

Loss is terrible for us to go through. Loss of a home, a partner, a job, or a pet are all deeply tearful times. But if the home we lost becomes freedom, and the partner is one we have outgrown, this is not loss even though it feels that way at the time. And then there is that job we hated. We never liked it, but we were too afraid to quit. Our troubles were over when we got fired. Thank God something got us out of there. Now we can hopefully be willing to find a job we love. If a loved one or good friend or a pet must go on ahead of us, it is hard. We are left behind, but we get to see how it is done. We get to know that life does go on. And with loss comes a reality that we all are here for a short time and we need to honor the moments and make the best of it. Mortality sets in and for this we can be grateful so that we stop wasting time and start showing up to all we love in the moment.

Gratitude is all of the above. As we grow and learn and show up we get to be grateful in the moment. It's like cutting the grass or painting a room…we receive instant gratification and who does not like that? Be grateful every step of the way and when you cannot be grateful at least acknowledge that you may understand more someday and this is another way of being grateful.

Chapter Thirteen

Being the Spiritual Gift YOU Are Meant to Be

WHEN WAS THE LAST TIME you asked yourself 'why am I here and what am I to do?' Many of us have asked but we forgot to listen and when we did, we thought that the information was for someone else...or was it? When fear of moving forward sets in because of doubt, we are unintentionally putting our life on hold. We are not judged in any way for this. However, we have slowed down our progress, and we are not getting where we could be. Fortunately, we can ask as many times as we want until we are ready to listen and then show up.

Emotional Rags to Spiritual Riches is not something we get or is handed off to us without our consent. We must consent to willingness and fearlessness as we move closer to finally accepting that we have Emotional Rags that can take us to Spiritual Riches. There are many, and the best ones are always yet to come once we begin to heal. Healing takes time but beginning to heal is where the first sign of coming gifts start showing up.

It is my hope that by sharing Universal Wisdom in a simple form that I call BLUE COLLAR SPIRITUALITY that all of us can take away some of these principles in this philosophy and use them by doing the next right thing in their life.

Retaining some of these principles in this short, simple book there will lead to a noticeable life change. It does not take long to see or feel the changes.

When it comes to changing our lives and thoughts we seem to exhibit a short term memory. But it is not a discouraging process as our short term memory loss will be startled and with a lesson in change and we will remember what we have decided to change. Doing things over and over does get the same results. The sanity returns once we are tired of being sick and tired of a behavior that no longer serves us. At that time we return to reasonable sanity and we are reasonably willing to get on with a healthier life. It will take practice. Fear no longer controls us emotionally, and if it does BLUE COLLAR SPRITUALITY comes with the gift of simplicity, which is what we are here to celebrate and have as full benefits for this life. Putting our time in proves that the rewards are endless.

It is helpful to know that we are not in a contest. We are not being graded. But patiently the Universe awaits our soulful acceptance and recognition that we can easily access the good we are here to have and to share. When we do, we are faced with some wonderful realizations and at that time a clear message comes through. And the sages of old have all agreed that we must...must give away all that we have learned so that we can keep it. This is accomplished by showing up to our own sacred contract.

It is imperative that we learn not to compare, not to judge, but to allow resentments to go. Our fear levels need to be low and our energy levels will automatically soar. We will notice how tireless and capable we are of anything that comes our way. And as we show up to all that we are here to do, there will be no need to dramatize or complain. Instead, like the legend of the Phoenix, we will rebirth and soar knowing no fearful boundaries and seeing only opportunity on all of our new horizons.

In conclusion I would like to share another personal thought. At the end of all my classes I suggest and nudge the following. "If you can remember just one thing in this session that will make your life better, please remember one thought...Just show up to the next right thing and you will be amazed at the transformation in not only your thinking but your life experience. Keep showing up and you will be more than fine."

Showing up to life has the simple answer to all of our questions, and the rest will come in increments of time, right on time. We are children of the Universe,and we are meant to be here. Being here means we are to have a life that is co-created with the God of our understanding. It is a personal relationship that we get to have. Take it! Enjoy it! And keep showing up…to the next right thing in your life. It is an incredible, unforgettable ride.

Namaste

NOW YOU HAVE IT! DON'T LOSE IT

Fall of 2015 will be the final book to this trilogy of Spiritual Enlightenment. Look for: NOW YOU KNOW…LET'S GO!

CPSIA information can be obtained
at www.ICGtesting.com
Printed in the USA
FSHW011421260521
81676FS